PRAISE FOR *HORSES SPEAK OF GOD*

"You don't have to be smitten with horses to fall in love with this book, which is rich with self-awareness and insight, anchored in the realities of living with intention, reverence, and love."

–MEREDITH GOULD,

author of *Desperately Seeking Spirituality*

"'Sit deeply.' Thrown by her horse, Laurie Brock received that counsel from her riding instructor. 'Sit deeply and ride.' Brock's book centers the reader in the necessity of balance and breath, routine and repetition, in our physical existence, and our spiritual lives, as well. Her relationships with the horses she rides, grooms, and loves speak to our relationship with both the embodied and the transcendent. We cannot grow without persistent practice, whether as riders or people of faith. We have to show up to meet God the way Brock settles on her horse, ready to move together, to be as one."

–REV. MARTHA K. SPONG,

co-author of *Denial Is My Spiritual Practice*

"This is a beautiful meditation on belief, the holy, and the healing power of horses. This profound book not only helped me see the magic of animals in everyday life, but allowed me a better under-standing of my own faith journey."

–SILAS HOUSE,

author of *South*

"Laurie Brock takes common things—horses and humans, saddles and stirrups—and finds in them profound truths. This honest book will give you new insights into yourself and your relationship with all God's Creation—even if you've never once been on a horse."

–NURYA LOVE PARISH,
Executive Director, Plainsong Farm; Priest-in-charge,
Holy Spirit Episcopal Church

"I've seen books change lives. This one demonstrates the importance of nurturing faith with our whole selves, in work and play and relationships. Sometimes it's a pleasant canter. Sometimes it's a hard fall. All the time, it is holy."

–RACHEL G. HACKENBERG,
co-author of *Denial Is My Spiritual Practice*

"Laurie Brock writes with great depth and passion. She gives us a sense of how horses—powerful, beautiful animals—might teach us about ourselves and about God."

–REV. CANON SCOTT GUNN,
Executive Director, Forward Movement

HORSES

SPEAK

OF GOD

*How Horses Can Teach Us to Listen
and Be Transformed*

LAURIE M. BROCK

PARACLETE PRESS
BREWSTER, MASSACHUSETTS

2018 First Printing

Horses Speak of God: How Horses Can Teach Us to Listen and Be Transformed

Copyright © 2018 by Laurie M. Brock

ISBN 978-1-61261-929-3

The Paraclete Press name and logo (dove on cross) are trademarks of Paraclete Press, Inc.

Library of Congress Cataloging-in-Publication Data:

Names: Brock, Laurie M., author.
Title: Horses speak of God : how horses can teach us to listen and be transformed / Laurie M. Brock.
Description: Brewster, MA : Paraclete Press, Inc., 2018. | Includes bibliographical references.
Identifiers: LCCN 2017057743 | ISBN 9781612619293 (trade paper)
Subjects: LCSH: Human-animal relationships–Religious aspects. | Horses–Religious aspects–Christianity. | Spirituality–Christianity.
Classification: LCC BV4596.A54 B75 2018 | DDC 248.8/8–dc23
LC record available at https://lccn.loc.gov/2017057743

10 9 8 7 6 5 4 3 2 1

Published by Paraclete Press
Brewster, Massachusetts
www.paracletepress.com

Printed in the United States of America

Dedicated to all the people who have the serenity to accept the things we cannot change, the courage to change the things we can, and the wisdom to know when to go ride a horse.

And to Nina.

A . . . woman never looks better than on horseback.

—GEORGE ELIOT IN *DANIEL DERONDA*

*The wind of heaven is that which blows
between a horse's ears.*

—ARABIAN PROVERB

CONTENTS

INTRODUCTION

$\mathcal{I}$ have a love affair with horses and their way of communicating.

Horses, while quite capable of vocalizations, particularly around feeding time, communicate more readily through their bodies. They respond to pressure. Their eyes, nostrils, and ears speak paragraphs about their thoughts and feelings. They paw at the ground with their hooves to communicate boredom or anxiety or, "Hey, give me a treat!" They sense subtle changes in a rider's stress or body position, sometimes even before the rider is aware of these fluctuations.

This love of horses was not instantaneous. My love affair with them was far more inconsistent, like the characters in a Jane Austen novel who engage and depart from one another over decades before recognizing the love of their life. My first horse ride was as a three-year-old on my grandparents' mare. I rode sporadically, filling my time in other ways. I rode again in college, then fell into the words of law school and later seminary.

Until one day I listened to God tell me something was missing in my life.

I ignored these words at first. I was paying my bills and was part of a wonderful church community.

God kept talking, as she does when we ignore the holy words directing us into a new place. And I listened long enough to find myself on the back of a horse, learning to feel its movements. Until one day when I discovered horses were attune to my feelings, even ones I wanted to suppress. Until one day when they felt truthful. They resonated in the body of my soul.

After I'd been riding regularly for a few months, I arrived at the barn early for my weekly lesson. I'd been at the bedside of a beloved parishioner who was making her great journey from life to death to eternal life. The church roof was leaking again, and I'd ended a relationship by breaking my own heart to be true to myself, an elegant way of saying it wasn't him, it was me . . . and who I was with him. As I walked into the barn, I encountered one of the grooms who asked me how I was.

"Fine," I replied, mincing my words.

I haltered Delilah, a black Friesian mare, and began the process of readying her for our ride. I brushed her. I picked her massive hooves, and I picked up a comb to brush her mane, snarled from a day out in the paddock.

And I cried. I wept in anger at the implications of loving others even unto death, of a roof leak, of the pain of endings. Of all that too often seems unfair about human life. I sobbed because I was not fine, and Delilah didn't have to ask me. She knew.

"Why can't life always feel joyful?" I prayed to God.

God responded, I think, with an eye roll.

I cried even more. The dust from Delilah's coat mixed with my tears, and I kept combing.

Delilah stood still as I used her mane to wipe away my tears. Friesian manes are slightly less absorbent than Kleenex tissues, but in the middle of a barn and in the midst of life, we use what we have to dry our tears.

I tacked her up and climbed on. After days of praying last rites and explaining why a relationship wouldn't work, I rode in silence and felt the most healing language I'd heard in days.

The language of healing that only horses speak.

And I realized that it is because of this language—because of the words of truth, of faith, of love, and of God that these horses had taught me—that I loved horses more than my own limited words could express, more than reason and intellect could explain.

These creatures teach me to feel life and faith in my body and in my being, not to cover these feelings with words and intellect. They push me to silence my brain and let my body feel. They feel my soul's emotions often before I do and entice me to experience my own emotions.

As I stepped Delilah up to a trot and felt my soul shift and balance on her, I breathed that deep breath out.

And I began to listen.

Words

*In the beginning was the Word, and the Word was
with God, and the Word was God.*

—JOHN 1:1

I have a love affair with words. I love the words
of Shakespeare's soliloquies and the Gospel of Luke's Song
of Mary. I love the way preachers weave together mundane
words into extraordinary insights about God. The poetry that
meanders into the human spirit and the hymns that sing out
from our souls ignite me. I caress the ramblings of ancient
theologians and modern mystics. I grew up with the words of
the Southern ghost stories of my ancestors while sitting on front
porches drinking iced tea as a fan angled over a bowl of ice
cooled the Southern summers.

I grew into a faith that loves words. The Episcopal Church
centers upon the Bible and the Book of Common Prayer. We
pray, listen, and sing words that span eons as we worship God.
Each Sunday I hold in my hands these words of salvation and

love. They have etched themselves into the memory of my self and soul as I pray the words of the Holy Eucharist.

"This is my body. This is my blood," the words of Jesus remind us.

"I give you a new commandment, to love as I have loved you;" we hear Jesus's words call us into a life of discipleship.

"Let us pray the words our Lord Jesus Christ taught us," as we begin the Lord's Prayer.

Words convey, share, witness, and tell.

So, you can imagine my surprise when, over coffee with a longtime friend as I processed the aftermath of my presence as a volunteer chaplain to law enforcement officers in the midst of the death of a young police officer, I had a very short response to one of her questions that involved horses.

We'd talked for well over an hour. I shared my own deep grief over this experience. I recounted the moments that stayed with me from the events, and the feelings from past traumas in my life that this current one unearthed. She listened, not making any comments and, especially helpful, not trying to make this tragedy have some deep meaning I wasn't ready for it to hold.

After some long, appreciated silences, she wondered out loud what in me moved myself and soul to stop what I was doing, answer the call from the police chief, and, in uncertainty and fear, go.

In past years, I would have had excellent answers. Because someone has to go, and I have training in this area. Because I was asked. Because it's what I signed up for. Some good words, and all things many of us would say when asked why we helped another in need. Some busy words that crowded out the silence so I wouldn't have to sit with the shifts and movements of my soul when life trembles like an earthquake through changes and chances and the unknown.

We humans, we lovers of words, prefer a constant narrative, with the words running from one edge of the page to another, and then from top to bottom, leaving no empty space for what is being held in the silence of emotion.

But this time, something else had shifted. I traced the rim of my cup of coffee and said, "Because I ride Izzy."

One of my volunteer ministries in my community is serving as a chaplain for my city's police department. I, along with other clergy of various denominations, make up a response team of chaplains available to those who have received the news that a spouse has died in a car wreck, a son has overdosed, or some other trauma has burst into their lives, shattering the thin veil of control many of us cultivate with our routine and plans.

Several weeks ago, I was washing the dishes that had rested a few too many days in the sink when my phone rang. Could I come to the hospital, because a police officer in a nearby town had been fatally shot? Law enforcement from all around were gathering and, surely, I'd know what to do.

No. That one word echoed within me for several moments after I hung up the phone.

No, not a young man dead. No, I don't know what to do.

But I went, and over the course of several hours, I offered my presence with prayers, by handing out tissues to stoic officers, and by standing with a community in the chaotic moments that remind us just how tenuous the façade of control in our lives truly is.

When any of us are present in these moments of profound change, this movement of a loss of control, a loss of the plans, ideas, and even rules we imagine our lives follow, whether our own or others, the experience shifts and repositions the pieces of our lives. Some adjustments are directly related to the event, but more often, we discover that other aspects of our souls have changed, too. The presenting event pulls back the curtain on other things in my life that had shifted and changed.

How did I stand in that almost-overpowering grief with hundreds of officers and be present with them?

Because I ride Izzy.

My friend looked at me, wondering if there would be more to come. I shook my head, "No." I could have tried to explain, but I knew the feeling, the moment, all that Izzy had taught me about losing control and having courage in a way no other teacher, self-help book, or certificate program could.

Chris, one of the owners and trainers of Wingswept Farm, where I ride, uses a paraphrase of a quote attributed to Mario Andretti when he talks about riding more challenging horses. He says that if you don't feel like you're about to lose control, you're not riding the best you can.

When I first began riding, that feeling of losing control of the horse, that feeling that the horse's trot was this close to getting out from under me, and I was going to be taken for a ride instead of directing the ride, was quite low. And God forbid if the horse broke gait and went from a trot to a canter when I wasn't ready. That was a sure recipe for me to clamp down on the reins, lean too far forward, and desperately grasp for control.

Thankfully, the horses I rode at this point in my riding career were quite trustworthy and calm. What felt like I was riding on the edge of losing control was actually far from that moment. The more I rode, however, the more spirited and energetic the horses became.

Then I met Izzy.

Izzy, with her energy, her attitude, and her vitality, was the first horse with whom I remember having that feeling of riding at the edge of losing control. I finally felt that moment Chris talked about, the moment I felt as if I were just on the very edge of losing control of a gait, while still riding. The emotions that shift and churn in that moment, those of confidence, some fear, some stupid courage, and great faith, aren't easily explained. They are seen in the horse. They are felt by the rider. They are experienced, and they become the voice of holy, ancient wisdom that Izzy shared with me.

As I reflected on the moment when I'd walked away from my dirty dishes and into the midst of tragedy in the aftermath of a death, I knew they were the same emotions, similar experiences.

I could be in the presence of grief and its wildness because I rode Izzy.

And suddenly, I realized that the rearranging that happened inside of my soul had to do with the words that horses had opened to me.

Not new words, but a new depth and significance to familiar words of faith. Richer, more intense words that pushed beyond the definitions I'd attributed to them over the decades. Words that stood at the edge of losing control. Words that moved far beyond the language of the intellect that explains and organizes and seeks to understand at a certain level.

I'd had an intensely familiar relationship with these words through the years. They had invited me to hold my faith within my hands and turn it upside down and inside out to examine it from different angles. I'd engaged the centuries of writings on God and the human experience with God, following these words in their questions and wandering in the desert to seek the answers.

"Because I ride Izzy," came from a transformed understanding of words. She'd opened a new complexity of words to me. The words I'd used for decades had a staircase leading to another level, and a door beyond that, and a trail beyond that door that meant I had to get on a horse to explore further. I hadn't been aware I'd wandered into this new place until I said four simple words out loud.

Yet those words held overwhelming meaning that had taken me time to feel and find the courage to vocalize and just the moment to say out loud. Coffee and trauma provided the moment.

These words speak to a primal emotion and embodiment and love that isn't explained but experienced. They are the language that collapses in heaves and incomplete breaths when we claw our way through deep, life-changing grief. This is the raw language we feel when we wake up on the floor in our own vomit and realize we will indeed live, but aren't sure yet how, and get up, clothed in shame and God's love, and go to the nearest twelve-step meeting. This language twists and turns in our guts when we are looking at an opportunity that seems good on paper, but something . . . something . . . doesn't make our heart sing.

God speaks in the language of reason in our intellect, but then God also speaks in the language of elegant and untamed emotion in our bodies.

I'd been slowly rediscovering the holy language of my body over the past years.

In the years I'd been riding, I'd often experienced horses and my interactions with them as an escape from routine, a place where I could be fully in my body and less focused on rambling, busy thoughts. But this was a new moment.

As I thought about my words capturing the moment of why I entered the space of grief, of deep turmoil, and of unwanted change because of a tragic death, I let the words I'd said over coffee echo.

Because I ride Izzy.

Riding her didn't give me particular skills in being present with grief. Riding her had given me courage accented with humility. Riding her made me admit my fear and saddle up anyway. And riding had, over time, given me a new way to experience and express thoughts and feelings and to understand words of faith in a deeply visceral way, a complex, holy shorthand for a vocabulary of faith spoken best by these animals that have intrigued, inspired, and humbled humans for eons.

The vast Word of God speaks to us in silence, in sound, in motion, in emotion, in sight and smell, and in art. Our Orthodox sisters and brothers take the sensuality of God through art to a particularly breathtaking level with the practice of praying with icons, a prayer practice that has thankfully seeped into the wider Christian world.

Icons are a type of religious art depicting Jesus, Mary, saints, angels, and holy moments like the Annunciation or the Resurrection. While certainly beautiful art, icons are used as a way to focus prayer. We pray with icons, not to them. I have an icon of saints Florus and Laurus surrounded by horses that gives my prayers form and focus.

I know about Florus and Laurus only because they have a holy connection with horses. I saw the icon in a store, the horses drawing my attention before the images of the two men. After I brought the icon home, I explored the story of these two men. They were twin stonemasons who lived in the second century. They were contracted to build a pagan temple and, after they built it, they consecrated it as a Christian church by gathering the Christians in Illyria (modern-day Albania and Croatia), destroying all the pagan images, erecting a cross, and praying without ceasing overnight in the now-Christian church.

This, as one can imagine, did not please the men who wanted a pagan temple built. In response to this act, the man who funded the pagan temple and his friends burned to death all the Christians who had prayed in the church and tossed Florus and Laurus down a well and buried them alive.

I wondered where horses came into this story. Did horses miraculously save Florus and Laurus from certain death?

No, actually. That's why they are martyrs. Because they died for their Christian faith.

Somewhere in this story, the archangel Michael visited the brothers and taught them the language of horses and the art of horsemanship, apparently before their unfortunate encounter with a well. A further legend tells that their bodies were found incorruptible and, on the same day, a deadly horse plague in the area ended. Thus, they are in some parts of the world the patron saints of horses and those who ride horses.

The archangel Michael taught them the language of horses. That moment is depicted in the icon with Michael in all his angelic splendor handing an ancient version of a lead shank to the brothers, allowing them to connect physically to the horses. This physical connection is necessary to understand the language of horses.

Horses understand human words. In the saddle-seat world, we are encouraged to talk to our horses as we ride. A soothing, calm, "Whoa, walk," is necessary to a particularly energetic horse to encourage and maintain a flat walk. We use words to call for the trot and the canter, and use verbal cues like kissing sounds and clucking sounds to speed up or slow down at these gaits.

I, however, discovered something else about their words, that they understood. Horses, I realized, had helped me understand the Word, the personification of God in the language of faith, which includes emotions, art, song, and silence.

Later that night, as I lit a candle in front of the icon of the two original horse people who listened to the language of horses, I allowed the sadness of the past days to have the space it needed in my soul, and I also began to marvel at the new language I had learned, imperceptively at first.

I began to ride as a hobby. I did not expect to learn a language that spoke of God. But Izzy's words helped me understand the moment of walking forward in faith and life, knowing that control is tentative and faltering, but that living and riding with any sort of existence means we walk right up to the verge and let our feet go beyond the threshold of comfort into the unknown. We cede our illusion of full control and are present to that moment.

I wondered what other words I'd learned, what other embodiments of God horses had spoken to me. When I rode, I felt excitement and challenge. A few times I could almost imagine an angel touching the reins as I rode, because the feeling was simply that ethereal.

And still other times I left the barn in tears feeling as if my soul had been tossed down the depths of a well and smothered with dirt. That feeling can come because my week has been long and arduous, and some moment of my ride slides the last brick out of the tenuous stack, and all the emotions come tumbling down. That feeling can also come because a horse gets the best of me, and I'm frustrated with my own limits as a rider.

Admitting I am still learning as a Christian and as a rider is humbling, and some days I don't want to be humbled. Horses, however, don't care and share that with me, too.

But horses do share with me, almost every time I ride, their words of God in their artistic and imaginative ways, ways my human language simply cannot do.

They speak, as only they can, the holy language God speaks to my deepest soul.

Movement

Heavenly Father, in you we live and move and have
our being: We humbly pray you so to guide and
govern us by your Holy Spirit, that in all the cares
and occupations of our life we may not forget you, but
may remember that we are ever walking in your sight;
through Jesus Christ our Lord. Amen.

—COLLECT FOR GUIDANCE,
The Book of Common Prayer

Drop your hips! Follow the movement of the horse!" I heard one of my riding instructors yell from the fence.

I was riding my horse on this Monday after Easter. My body was still that strange mixture of exhausted adrenaline most clergy experience after Holy Week. Twelve church services in one week have that impact on a body. I'd asked Nina, my sassy, elegant chestnut horse, to canter, but the viscous residue of the past week caused me to bounce more in the saddle than I should while riding a canter.

Riding is a strange dance of stillness, balance, and movement. The horse moves, and the rider follows the movements of the horse with parts of her body and is at the same time still with other parts. It's a unique form of aerobic meditation. These movements are assisted by tack: bridles and reins allow us to communicate through our hands with the horse's head and mouth. Want the horse to go right or left? Gently move the reins that way, unless the horse doesn't respond; then pull harder. But be careful not to pull too hard, or the horse can get mad. Getting in a fight with your horse never ends well for either human or horse. Strive for steady hands, keeping them still but firm, mostly using your fingers and wrists to direct the horse. Tiny human appendages direct a ton of an animal.

We ride in a saddle, which allows us to communicate to the horse through our seat and legs. On some horses, I use my legs more than my hands to guide. Horses respond to pressure. Pushing my right leg onto the side of the horse will move the horse away from the pressure. But don't push your feet into the horse's sides too much, because that's a signal to go faster. Sit deep in the saddle. Listen to how the horse is responding to all the cues and aids with legs, seat, and hands, and adapt accordingly.

This is riding, a strange dance indeed.

Riding also, obviously, involves a horse. All horses have three basic gaits: the walk, the trot, and the gallop. Different breeds of horses have some variations of these gaits due to selective breeding for their uses throughout history. Saddlebreds, the main breed I ride, are known for their trots, exuberant and big.

Saddlebred trainer Smith Lilly describes a trot as "a two-beat gait in which each diagonal pair of legs (right front—left hind or left front—right hind) moves together in an even rhythm."[1] A horse's trot can be a smooth and even gait or energetic and lofty, barely contained, or somewhere in between. Sometimes the same horse can have all that variety in her trot in one day. Either way, riding a trot in my discipline is called posting a trot. Posting is the movement developed by employees of the British Postal Service in the eighteenth century to make riding long distances on bouncing, trotting horses more comfortable for horse and rider.

And instead of sitting in the saddle as the horse moves, I rise and fall with each step. Up. Down. Up. Down. Up. Down. On the right diagonal, my body rises out of the saddle as the horse's leg along the fence rail or arena wall moves forward. Riding a trot in the post allows the movement of the horse to send you upward into the post, and gravity to bring you back down into the saddle. Strength in core and legs gives the rider control, so we move with the moment of the horse. In fact, a way to slow down a horse in the trot is to slow down my post. My horse feels my movement and responds.

We also ride a canter, which is essentially a very collected, controlled gallop. To call for the canter, we stop the horse, tip her head gently to the rail and apply pressure with the leg next to the rail, and make a kiss sound or say, "Canter." The tip to the rail and the leg pressure shifts the horse's body and gets the horse to canter on the correct leading leg; this helps her balance—and by extension, the rider's balance. A canter is a horse equivalent to a human jog. We move forward, but not at a speed that is alarming, like people running from creepy clowns. Horses prefer to gallop if they want to move quickly, perhaps fleeing from a predator in the wild. My horse Nina prefers to nap. Domestic life agrees with her.

While posting a trot is an up-down movement, riding a canter is a deep seat in which the rider follows the movement of the horse with the hips. The rider's backside never leaves the saddle, or at least that's the ideal. Riders follow the rocking movement of the canter through our legs and our hips while the upper part of our body stays quiet and steady. The upper part of the body should not rock, while the lower half does. If our hands move forward and backward with the horse's head, she's likely to use that movement to pick up speed. Perfect for a fast gallop, not so much for a canter.

With all this blend of movement and balance in our seat, core, and legs, our hands on the reins should be quiet, soft, and steady as they communicate with the horse. In my formation as a priest, we were taught to listen to those who come to us with problems and questions. Come to think of it, every caring human being has to learn to do this. To listen, I have to be quiet, I have to sit still. I can't imagine how well I would communicate, "I hear you," to someone sharing with me her trauma of finding out the diagnosis is cancer as I rearranged my bookshelf or vacuumed the carpet.

A rider's hands communicate with a horse the same way. When I hold them softly but firmly, I let the horse know I'm there and what I want her to do. When I am still with my hands, my horse is able to talk to me and tell me what she's thinking about doing, and I'm able to talk to her by telling her what I'd like her to do. If she drops her head, I feel it. If I want her to trot a circle, a movement in my hand guides her mouth and thus her head and her body. I have a tendency to have busy hands. I should make my instructor a sign to hold up when I ride that says QUIET HANDS, so she can save her voice.

We in the saddle-seat discipline (that's what we call the style of riding with which I'm involved) do all this in the bare remnants of a saddle. It's not much more than a racing saddle that jockeys use with nicer nameplates on the back. Western saddles are made to hold the rider, ropes, a few saddlebags, if needed, and a steamer trunk and other supplies needed to trek across country herding cattle or chasing outlaws. The saddle I use, a variation on English saddles, is called a cutback; it was made to hold a rider, but barely.

It looks more like a potato chip covered in leather.

All these movements demand that I be aware and listening, both to me and to the horse. I love that even at the walk, which seems so basic, I am still asked to pay attention to movement. Is the horse flat walking? Is the horse jogging, which is a jazzy, animated walk? How is my body position when the horse walks? Am I tense?—that will be communicated to the horse and likely not result in a very relaxed walk. Am I relaxed but not sack-of-potatoes-in-the-saddle relaxed? Am I paying attention to the horse?

I don't jump horses over hedges, oxers, or walls. I did one time. The jump was maybe an inch off the ground. I may do it again one day, but at the moment I find great love and challenge in riding horses in the saddle-seat style. I love the blend of movement and stillness that is riding a horse. I love listening to the horse tell me at what speed she looks her best at the trot and to feel how slowly I can encourage her to canter. I love talking to horses with nothing but feel and movement and stillness through a leather potato-chip saddle. I love this bewitching dance between horse and rider that is saddle-seat riding.

Riding is a constant series of moments of change. Some of the moments of change we control. One sixty-degree afternoon, the kind that delights both horse and rider on a flawless autumn day in Kentucky, I ask Nina, my very own Saddlebred horse, to step up into the trot and transition down to the walk. I call for the canter. I ask her to canter a circle or trot a figure eight. I communicate this change to her.

Some of the acts of change I don't initiate. If Nina is convinced there is a horse-eating monster in the corner of the arena and spooks when we go down to the far corner, jumping sideways, I respond to her movement, first by holding on and second by suggesting to her she's going to trust to me and ride into the corner of the arena because I'm adept at protecting her from horse-eating monsters in the arena.

Movement and change are inherent to riding horses. To remain stiff and fixed is a sure way not to enjoy a ride, for either the horse or the rider. When I get stiff and rigid during a ride, I'm almost always anxious. The horse responds to my anxiety by trotting faster than needed, by not walking, or by not listening to my cues. Then I respond unhelpfully by engaging in too much movement—my hands become fidgety, my shoulders creep up to my ears, I lean forward, and get more rigid. I did this more in my early years of riding, as if rigidity is a helpful response to movement. Riding stiff is as helpful as wearing skinny jeans to a Thanksgiving dinner.

Lately, I'm getting better, maybe just marginally, but still better, with sensing the movement of the horse as a way of telling me to relax, to let muscles, tendons, joints, and spirit move. And when I don't do that well, my instructors' voices will always be a dependable backup.

"Relax!" they yell. "Drop your shoulders; loosen your hips! Sit deep!"

I'm amazed at how well we humans respond to verbal cues. We're like horses that way. Sometimes the verbal cue can remind us of the movement we need to allow and accept. Riding is movement of both rider and horse. The horse is not a stationary part of the relationship. She moves in all sorts of directions. Every part of her movement asks me to respond with movements, even when that movement is to steady myself. Every movement triggers my own muscles to engage or relax.

Our relationship with God, and by extension, our community of other people, is one of moment. We shift and change. Other people walk forward, run back, and stop moving. And God moves.

We too often forget that God is alive and moving. Yes, God is steadfast, but steadfast is not mixed in concrete, set into cold permanence, and displayed behind glass. God is incarnate flesh and blood in Jesus, who lived and moved.

He walked over dusty roads. He walked on water. He sat with people and ate. He prayed. He moved through holy places to teach and heal and turn over tables. Jesus was filled with movement. And yet, we are often guilty of the sin of making Jesus into an idol, cast only in stone and jewels and metal, fixed in one place as we live and move and have our being in the life away from Christ.

Nope. Jesus moves with us. Jesus, being God and all that goes with that, even moves us. Our faith needs movement, flexibility in the tendons and muscles that hold it together. And yet we humans are remarkably inflexible in matters of faith and life. We forget that movement and change are aspects of living things.

Change is that word that so many faithful people embrace intellectually and reject emotionally. We think we are the only ones ever in the history of faith who have been called to change.

"Not so," we hear the apostle Paul exhort us from the pages of his letters.

Paul is a paragon of the faith of a God of movement. A faithful Jewish man who persecuted those who followed Jesus, he was good at persecuting, likely because he was convinced to his core that he was right and these new Jesus followers were wrong.

How much courage did he have to move from that place to one of becoming a disciple of Christ? He had first to admit he was wrong and stiff-necked. Then he had to wait, blindly, for God through humans to reveal a new vision. The steadfast faith of Paul's witness to movement can be read in his letters. Read them from the first (First Thessalonians) to the last (Romans), and witness where he balances, where he shifts, and how he comes to understand God who constantly creates and re-creates and who affirms the ways to love that reflect God's love for us and offers us more expansive ways to love that will likely ask us to change.

How do we react when God through humans asks us how we are willing to change? When we hear the word *change*, do we get physically and emotionally stiff?

Change?

Yes.

Change.

Maria, another Saddlebred horse I love riding, excels at teaching me lessons in growth and change. I spent quite a few months fearful when I rode her because of her tendency to reply to my unhelpful riding habits by trotting or cantering faster than helpful to either of us. Our first show together, she picked up the pace of our trot to a not quite Kentucky Derby speed, but not much slower.

I did not feel on the verge of being out of control. I felt very much out of control.

But I kept riding her, kept listening to her, kept growing and changing as her movements jolted me out of rigidity and into flexibility. I listened if she picked up speed, her way of telling me I was sitting too far forward and to sit up and sit deep or to be gentle with the reins. I listened to my instructors. I realized that to grow as a rider, I couldn't stay where I had been. I had to change.

To grow as people of faith, we must move from where we are to where God is calling us to be, to lose a bit of control, and that will inevitably only happen through change.

Change. Movement. Growth.

Those are the hallmarks of God, and our embodiment of them is a reflection of God. We read that the Spirit of God moved over the face of the chaos of the world in the beginning of creation. The people of God move between fixed points, from Egypt to the Promised Land, from the Upper Room to Golgotha to the mountaintop where Christ ascended (moved) to sit at the right hand of God. In all these movements, things changed. What had been became something else. We cannot open our hands to receive God's new gifts and at the same time clench our hands closed to hang on to the past.

A term the writers of the Bible use to capture the essence of being averse to God's movement is *stiff-necked.* Our vision is cast in one direction, usually one we have picked because we like the view. We cannot or will not move. We become riders with the bad habits of leaning forward, sitting as if we are cast in cement, and grabbing the reins with all muscle and no finesse and wondering why our horses don't cooperate.

I suspect change in and of itself isn't fearful, but when it comes with loss, as it often does, that stirs a deep reaction. We cling to what we know, what has become familiar, even when what is familiar and known is not life-giving. We worry that change means we were wrong before. Maybe we were wrong, or maybe we were right with the information and experience we had at the time, but now we know more.

When we know more, when we experience a different viewpoint, when we have our vision changed, God loves us into movement. God loves us in our willingness to walk into newness of love.

Riding a horse is not about inflexibility; it's about movement, both the horse's and the rider's. Riding is responding to the other, feeling cues when movements are not aligned, and feeling that perfect moment of collaboration when it all works together. This dynamic stillness allows me to feel the horse's movement. If I'm fighting, fidgeting, and rigid, I may seem still from the outside, but I'm not.

I cannot be a good rider if I'm stiff-necked.

And yet I often try to be a good Christian by being stiff-necked. Stiff-necked may look firm in faith, fixed in Jesus, and grounded in God, but it's not. It's simply humanity being stubborn. It's humans arguing with God that our vision and understanding of God is the correct one, the one we're going to use to guide our way through life, and our yelling that our understanding of God cannot ever change.

This isn't to say that tradition isn't important. It is. Tradition anchors us to the wisdom of the past. When, however, we only look to the past for insight about God and how we love and serve each other, we are stiff-necked. Do we cling to our tradition as our excuse not to change, not to move? Do we cling to our desire to be right, or are we willing to change when we learn another way?

Our faith is a steadfast faith of stillness, balance, and movement. Part of our life in Christ is asking ourselves the question, "Where is God moving me now?" Countless followers of God and Christ have asked this question, sometimes with firm conviction, but mostly with shaking voices. Faith is the willingness to be changed, to be proven wrong about what we have believed or to realize what we have held on to about any number of things is no longer helpful. A living faith is my responding to God's movements and even God responding to mine. A living faith is steadfast but not stiff-necked. A living faith moves with life, change, hope, and grace.

As with riding a horse, it's not always easy to follow the movements of a living faith. But when we pay attention to the movements of God, when we are aware and listening, we move with God, we grow with God, and we change more and more into the people God has called us to be.

Steadfastness

*Spoiled horses, difficult horses, and even rogues, can
teach us much that is important; the rider who is too
well mounted may never really learn to ride.*
—WILLIAM STEINKRAUS,
"RIDING AND JUMPING"[2]

wanted an easy horse: one who did what I asked
with little effort, one who didn't have many opinions of her own,
and one who offered little challenge to me. One who, honestly,
didn't make me work very hard while I was riding. I was not in
the mood for movement, either mine or the horse's. I wanted
sure and certain.

That's because my spirit was not in an easy place. I was
challenged in the love-your-neighbor arena at that moment and
annoyed that I'd signed on to this following-Christ life.

More so than I usually am.

Fantasy faith is easy. We gather with people who are nice, who tell us we are nice, and who sing all the same songs we do with zest, fervor, and in perfect pitch. We like people who like the same worship styles. We hang out with those who vote for the same political candidates that we do. We agree on all the same sins. Our confession of sins follows the format of the person who sinned against us saying, "Oh, I'm sorry," and we reply with a gentle, "No, no, that's okay."

We read the Bible, except only the portions that fuel our fantasy faith of nice and sweet. The Nativity story in Luke, when read only on the surface, fits that standard. Angels, shepherds, sheep, and a sweet baby seem easy. And when Jesus talks about love it seems easy, but only if we make sure not to read the entire teaching about love. We've become adept at bypassing the hard reality of love.

No one ever says anything critical of us, and certainly not God. We come to worship, pray, and sing, and God says to us, "Good job!" as we walk out into the world, affirmed in our ease.

Fantasy riding is easy, too. I pet horses and feed them peppermints. I sit in the saddle on an easy horse and ride around the arena hearing, "Good job!" as I walk, trot, and canter. It's the calm trail ride where nothing interesting happens. I could ride the horse and read a novel all at the same time. The horse will never do anything surprising or annoying. And at the end of it all, I get a blue ribbon.

Easy.

Never mind that hearing, "Good job!" when our ease is being affirmed allows us to stay in stasis, allows us to fix and set the idols of our perfect selves and ignore the reality of our imperfect selves. Easy faith is a fun-house mirror that distorts our perceptions. We can be seduced by easy faith, translating the presence of all is calm and all is bright to perfect faith and the presence of the winds of chaos and upheaval as the absence of God.

As if the story of God and God's interaction with humanity is one long epic narrative of calm and easy, with all the good things in life fixed and set in permanent visions of sunshine and unicorns.

Remaining fixed and set, for all its attractiveness, perhaps even for all its similarity in our minds to the holy concept of steadfastness, is not helpful to riding a horse or living a life of faith. It's a fantasy of ease that keeps us where we are, unable to shift, change, and grow. The fantasy of ease invites us to embrace the sin of thinking that we are perfect, with nothing left to learn.

That's certainly not true with me, and I doubt I'm that original to humanity. If that great writer of the Christian faith, the apostle Paul, has shifts and moves in his ideas of a life of Christ, certainly we—who have not been struck blind by God, imprisoned because of our belief, and become a paragon of the faith because of our evangelism—haven't gotten all our beliefs and understandings about God correct on the first, second, or three thousandth try.

But I wanted an easy horse today, and I wanted an easy God. One that didn't challenge me or ask my muscles of balance and faith to stretch and strain to the next place.

All my fantasies about an easy God disintegrate when I'm facing the challenge of forgiveness. At that moment, a member of the body of Christ, one who affirms the belief of our faith in the Nicene Creed and receives Eucharist on Sundays and holy days as I do, has angered me. I feel used and betrayed by someone I considered a friend.

My easy faith gives me all the permission I need to categorize him as a sinner, as someone who clearly has issues, and as someone I don't have to love. Easy makes itself known in either/ or dichotomies. Complexity, nuance, and compassion are all marks of the richness of a living faith, the faith of God in Christ.

Jesus, being the bothersome presence he frequently is in our lives, reminds me otherwise. Do I get to be angry with someone who says hurtful things about me and who betrays me? Yes. Do I get to reconsider how to be in a loving relationship with someone who is careless with words? Yes. Do I get to condemn him to the outer darkness where there is weeping and gnashing of teeth?

Well, I want to say, "Yes!" but Jesus puts his hand over my mouth to shut me up and reminds me that love and forgiveness are intermeshed, and I don't get to choose the easy, comfortable parts of what I may call love and ignore the parts that move me and ask me to grow and learn.

While I wanted an easy horse, when I arrived at the barn, smoldering in my anger, which by this time had become quite self-justified and high-handed, I saw that I was not riding an easy horse at all.

Not that I really ever get to do that anymore during a lesson. The bomb-proof horses, those who walk and trot with ease and never spook at imaginary things in corners, never get excited and go-go-go at the speed of light, or never get annoyed and try to deposit you on the ground, are reserved for beginning riders or types of lessons that involve no stirrups or no reins or no saddle—which, in case anyone wonders, are not easy lessons.

Rita is a good horse. She's simply not easy. She is fussy about her bit, and when she goes into a canter, she can turn into a thousand-pound pogo stick if her rider doesn't collect her with a focused gentleness. My first few times of riding her were far bouncier than I wanted them to be. She has bounced me right off her and right onto the ground.

Riding Rita's not-easy canter has taught me to keep my balance and sit centered and heavy. She has taught me how to have what is known as an independent seat. A seat is foundational for the rider, with our sit bones getting an equal distribution of weight. Our seat is anchored by the inner thighs and knees in constant contact with the saddle, a great way to develop inner thigh muscles and a sure way never to fit comfortably in skinny pencil skirts ever again. Riding thighs keep your seat the saddle. The more balanced riders are in the saddle, the more our thighs and knees keep us balanced, the more we are able to use our hands on the reins and our calves to communicate to the horse instead of to find ways to balance on the horse.

Rita's pogo-stick style can easily inform me how balanced I may or may not be in the saddle if I'm leaning forward and not sitting deeply in the saddle. She's sent me bouncing before, and it's not an experience I want to repeat today. She's taught me to keep a firm hold on the reins without pulling and while being ready to give when I feel her begin to bounce up and down. She has a sweet spot that works. Too little and she's galloping; too much and she bounces. She reminds me to encourage her to go forward with my legs while keeping her head and neck up. If I'm using my hands and calves to balance on her instead of the core muscles of my abs, thighs, and knees, she will inform me. All of those skills make me a better rider, no matter which horse I'm riding.

Rita, the not-easy horse, taught me how to do all these things before, and she teaches them to me on this particular day. Riding her is complex, not easy. I sit in the saddle on her, take my three deep breaths to release all the heaviness I'm carrying on this day, all the anger, frustration, fixed standards of perfection to which I hold myself and others that need to be shattered, and another dose of anger. I inhale the smells of hay, of shavings, and the holy smell of horses. And Rita and I ride.

Riding, for the many gifts it gives me, shifts me wholly into the present moment. Guiding a thousand-pound creature of God around the arena is not the time to consider a grocery list or the many things you'd like to say to someone who has harmed you and bruised your soul. And an interesting thing happens for me while I'm actively in the present moment instead of dwelling on fixing the patches of concrete of my hate and frustration.

I have a new perspective.

Our brains and souls need downtime to work at their best. Research shows that our brains need to be bored to be at our most creative and most reflective. This phenomenon called mind-wandering has huge implications for our own personal creativity, and I think it has implications for our religious creativity as well.

Research on boredom shows that this downtime is anything but. Our brains, in their complicated, mysterious way, move around in space and time, exploring random thoughts, memories, even problems in our lives, connecting ideas in new ways. Our brains engage in this creative processing when we are physically active in a familiar space or activity: doing the dishes, walking your dog, or maybe even riding a horse.

Boredom is not easy. If it were, we wouldn't flee from it so frantically by checking our smartphones with the speed of light at the first signs of it. Boredom is intricate and difficult because it holds within it the complexities of doing nothing and doing more than we are aware. It is, like all that is vast about God, almost so easy we feel too challenged to do it. Such is the mysticism of holiness, both simple and complex at the same time.

Riding horses is a mystical practice of boredom in the holiest way of being active. No, it's not the same boredom of staring into a campfire and doing nothing. I am riding an animal who has her own ideas about life and can express those ideas in ways that will send me thinking very rapidly about how to stay in the saddle. But it is a way to shut off the busy-busy-busy aspects of the overthinking brain. When I ride, I'm focused on the relationship between the horse I'm riding and me, and the other horses and riders in the ring with me. I scan my body from top to soles of feet.

The holy presence of riding forces me out of my head and my stuff, whatever weighty and even inconsequential stuff I've collected during the day, and into the compassionate presence of the horse. While all those questions seem to cloud riding, they don't. They are asked and answered, not in my head, but in my body. My brain is busy in a more primal way while another part of my soul gets to process for a while. As I ride Rita, I'm not agonizing about complexities of forgiveness and love. I'm settling into my body and focused on relaxed hands and knees rolled inward. As I call her to a trot, my mind focuses on looking upward, keeping her straight, and me not getting too high off the saddle as I post. I'm not stewing over my distasteful feelings toward another child of God or pondering what I'd like to do to that other child of God that may not be legal in most states. As I ask Rita to canter, I'm remembering all the things our not-easy rides of the past have taught me, and how we (mostly) make riding her canter look easy.

Of course, because good riding takes hard work, my instructor asks me to start again.

"Make the start cleaner," she instructs, asking me to pay attention more to my form, sit back, and be less dramatic with my hands as I call for the canter. "A gentle lift, not so sudden," she says.

We all need *easy* on occasion, a break, a time to catch our breath. But easy doesn't develop new muscles, new capabilities, or new understandings. Easy allows us to rest, even to be bored when we need to engage in that spiritual discipline. If we stay there too long, we become stiff and fixed. Steadfastness is not immovable; it is remembering our basics.

Steadfastness is not easy. In fact, it is the aspect of faith and life that allows us to move more freely, to find flexibility and change and move with it instead of fighting against it. I brush Rita after we've finished our ride. And I remember the events of the week.

Am I still angry? Yes, but I also know the steadfastness of love will allow me to maneuver through this initial anger and hurt into something I can learn. Anger as a response to someone's betrayal is appropriate, but what I do with that anger and pain is mine. Do I lash out, or do I find a way to love myself and God (and that person with whom I'm angry) through this place?

What we do with our pain is ours. Will I forgive? Yes, and I will not settle in the easy but unhelpful mantra of forgive and forget. Betrayal, words meant to hurt, even words not meant to hurt, all damage relationships. The cracks can rarely be plastered over as if they were never there. Forgiveness reminds us we can move past the ease of absolutes—I forgive you completely or I will never forgive—and into the complexities of forgiveness and love. I forgive you, and that forgiveness may be uncomfortable for a while as the relationship forms in this new place, even if that new place means we are not in a mutual relationship anymore, but are in relationship as fellow followers of Christ.

The many not-easy horses I've ridden and will continue to ride teach me moment by moment. I don't have to get in the saddle and be perfect. I simply have to get into the saddle and be willing. Because I am willing to ride horses who challenge me, I will be transformed and changed as a rider.

God asks the same of us. Are we willing? Are we willing to learn from our moments of difficulty and pain and from our moments of accomplishment? Are we willing to be bored and allow the holy parts of our souls to process and maneuver through events, or do we need to force ourselves into false solutions?

Are we willing, in our relationship with God and God's children, those who love us and those who anger us, to be challenged, to be changed, and to be transformed?

Fear

Do you give the horse its might? Do you clothe its neck
with mane? Do you make it leap like the locust?
Its majestic snorting is terrible. It paws violently,
exults mightily; it goes out to meet the weapons.
It laughs at fear, and is not dismayed;
it does not turn back from the sword.

—JOB 39:19–22

id you ask her to do that?" I heard Stephanie,
my instructor, ask across the arena. We both knew the answer to
her question.

I was riding my horse, Nina, an American Saddlebred. Nina
is a smart horse who enjoys thinking a few steps ahead of her
rider. She also enjoys taking advantage of riders if she senses
they aren't directing her. Or if they are directing her and she
senses an opening. Nina is an opportunist. She needs direction.
And I wasn't directing her. I wanted her to canter. She decided
a trot would be appropriate for the moment.

"No," I said. I had a few excuses to offer, but stopped. I was riding her, not the other way around. Anything she did was on me as a rider.

I like to say God introduced me to American Saddlebreds. American Saddlebreds are a truly American horse, even a truer Kentucky horse. They were bred from several horse breeds, including the now-extinct Narragansett Pacer and the Thoroughbred, beginning in the eighteenth century. Breeding continued to sharpen gaits and performance, and eventually the breed known as the American Saddlebred came to be recognized. The United States Equestrian Federation describes the breed, saying a Saddlebred "carries himself with an attitude that is elusive of description—some call it 'class,' presence, quality, style, or charm. This superior air distinguishes his every movement."[3] They are known as the peacock of the show ring.

These horses are not shrinking violets.

My experience tells me that riding them invites riders to step up. After all, a showy, fancy horse does not care for an apprehensive, shrinking rider.

I began my American Saddlebred riding life as an apprehensive, shrinking rider. I was still stumbling my way forward as an apprehensive first-time rector. My default nature in life was one of apprehension and shrinking. Much of my childhood and adolescence had been filled with a list of don'ts that reduced my self-confidence shred by shred. I countered that with a commitment to accolades and awards. If my inner self felt depreciated and reduced, apprehensive and fearful, I responded by piling all the accomplishments I could around me to hide behind them.

That only works for so long.

Eventually life happens, events happen, and God happens, and all the bricks of the protective wall crumble. While playing small felt easier than filling out my soul and having confidence, I'd discovered that if I continued to do so, I would fade away.

So, I found more and more of my voice, myself, and my soul. I thought I'd gotten accomplished at this deep simplicity of authenticity. Then I met Nina.

She introduced herself to me after I'd been riding Saddlebreds for about a year. Her owners were looking to sell her, and I was looking to buy my very own horse. The minute I rode her, I felt my inner seven-year-old self squeal with the joy that every little girl has when she gets her very own pony.

I didn't squeal with joy so much when, some months later, Nina deposited me into a fence. I'd just been feeling more confident as a rider when Nina and I hit this moment in our relationship. A horse kicked at her. She bolted. I came off her and fell into a fence. Five broken ribs, sixty days with no riding, and a new barn later, any confidence I had stayed shattered near the fence where I fell months ago.

I was—again—an apprehensive, shrinking rider.

I was afraid.

I didn't want to say the words out loud. To do so sounded like a reversion to a life I wanted to leave behind, a return to a skittish, fearful child who hid under the bed when her parents argued and who tried very, very hard to be worthy of love by acquiring a resume of accomplishments.

No matter how much we grow physically, our souls live eternally at all our ages at once. All the trauma, joy, and life of our younger years lives within our cells and memories. Growth physically doesn't mean we outgrow the heartache of our past. We may have more distance from what is within us or allow our present life to distract us, but the shadows of our past, especially those which cause us pain, do not disappear.

We don't simply outgrow our pain.

Instead, we grow into it. We birth it into our consciousness, our awareness, and we get to know it. Have tea with it. Or bourbon. Quit acting as if the parts of our tender souls that have been damaged and wounded by the hardships of life do not exist. So, when they tap us on our souls and say, "Hello," we don't scream and lash out at their surprising presence.

The apocryphal Gospel of Thomas accords this saying to Jesus: "If you bring forth what is within you, what you bring forth will save you. If you do not bring forth what is within you, what you do not bring forth will destroy you."[4]

We humans have a tendency to reach outward to heal our own wounds, not a most helpful practice. We think, perhaps, if we can fix another, we can fix ourselves. Or if we find the perfect job or perfect partner or perfect weight, we will find peace, calm, and happiness. For many years, I thought if I could help others be heard, if I could help others be unafraid, if I could help others find confidence, I would magically find all those same things.

I was shocked to discover that medicating someone else's wound did not have any impact on mine. Jesus offered me another option: to collaborate with God to heal the wounds within myself. Bring them forth into consciousness, and let the wounds and God's healing of them change me.

Jesus's wisdom is deep and simple, annoyingly so. I would rather have a much more complicated, intellectual approach than delve into my own soul wounds to be able to bring forth love into me that I can in turn share with the world. What is often the surface image of ourselves is the mask of an actor, the outward role we are trying to play; the deep truth of who we are requires some time to be birthed into awareness, mainly because it is painful to dig into wounds we've bandaged with rags and ignored for decades.

All those disappointments, damaging experiences, wounds, and heartbreaks from our past that reach into our present yearn to be brought forth and, with time and awareness, transformed by God.

Faith gives us courage to sit with our pain, with the anguish we've encountered in our lives, the experiences inflicted upon us and sometimes experiences we inflict upon ourselves, and bring them forth into our awareness. Not initially, perhaps, but as we allow our trust in God to guide us down those foreboding paths into our past, we discover what's there.

We bring them forth. We have permission to explore our pain and a promise from God that we do not walk alone through the valley of the shadow of death. Yes, healing will be unsettling and unsavory. We will probably have to let go of the security blanket of blame and helpless victimhood that keeps us stuck in powerlessness. And we may not be sure we will survive.

I wanted not to be afraid of riding, especially of riding my own horse. I tried to be fearless for a few months, to act as if I was comfortable in the saddle. I was not going to admit I was afraid.

I was not going to say out loud, "I am afraid of riding. I am afraid I'll get hurt again."

I didn't have to say the words. My instructor said them for me. "You are afraid," she observed as I sat on Nina. I'd angled her head to the fence so she would stop and I could sit on my horse, pause, and catch my breath because she was not doing what I wanted her to do. I could sit and pretend not to be afraid.

But I was.

Horses are amazing communicators. They pick up on the subtleties of our bodies and souls that we hide even from ourselves. I may have been thinking I was asking Nina to canter, but I was afraid she would bolt with me, so my body, probably subconsciously, was asking her not to canter. Mixed signals make for a confused horse, and with Nina, this was simply an opportunity to do exactly as she wanted.

Which added to my anxiety and fear.

As much as I didn't want to say the words aloud, I realized I needed to give myself permission to admit I was scared of riding, and especially scared of riding my own horse. Apprehensive and shrinking denial in the face of fear simply makes the fear grow like kudzu. Pretending not to be afraid is a lie. Feeling the fear is more courageous.

Fear is deep and simple; it's primal. We cover it with negativity when, in fact, fear likely has kept us alive as a species. Fear and its cousin, anger, are often our first clues that something may be threatening. Angels begin their encounters with humans in Holy Scripture with the words "Fear not," not because they are sweet, gentle beings bathed in holy light, but because they are unsettling, otherworldly creatures about to upend human plans. Moses, Mary, Joseph, Balaam's ass—all had their plans changed by encounters with God's angels. All had ideas of what life was going to be until an angel of God appeared and said, "Have I got an offer for you!"

Fear is a natural by-product of an event that changes us. Standing on the edge of something new with our toes hanging off the cliff is a fearful moment. Fear is often the shadow that allows the light of love, excitement, and newness to shine. My therapist once said those who say they are never fearful are either lying or dead inside.

What we do with fear can be death-dealing or life-giving. Too often we try to disown fear, snuff it out. Herod feared losing his power, so he ordered all the infants slaughtered to prevent the rise of the Infant King Jesus. We can fear losing something we are quite sure we cannot live without, and we may hold on so tightly that we smother all life out of something and preemptively kill the new creation God is hoping to birth in our lives.

Or we can speak our fear, acknowledge it, and recognize that it, too, is something of God. I'd spent the last few years feeling my fill of fear. I was fearful of what would happen if I allowed myself to feel angry about how the church had broken my heart. I was fearful of venturing forth into a new call in a new city and a new state. I was fearful about my own ability to be a rector in charge of a congregation.

I'd taken up riding, in some ways, to escape fear. And now, after a time of enjoying all that is horses, I found myself right back in the middle of all my fears. In our fear, we can refuse to move, crawling instead into the pain of our brokenness and staying there, a wounded creature unwilling to offer ourselves for healing or change. Even when healing has occurred, even when change has come, the residue of fear remains until we give ourselves permission to find our way to courage and confidence.

I wanted the grand moment when I didn't feel afraid of riding horses at all. Or when I didn't feel unsteady about preaching a sermon the Sunday after violence had taken the life again of another young man of color, of children in school, of partiers at a gay club. I wanted not to feel fearful when I buried a deeply loved member of my parish and wondered what will happen in the space her death leaves behind. I wanted not to feel fear when someone's personal demands of me felt counter to my authentic self and what would happen when I disappointed them to be true to me.

I wanted to make fear a sinful and evil thing that could be banished with the right prayers and seventy-two therapy sessions.

I wanted to be sure I'd never be hurt again, by horses or humans.

That did not happen. That will not happen.

But what did happen? My instructor told me to go back out and ride, to take up on the reins and sit deeply and ride. To ask my horse to do something and, in kind, to ask myself to do something. To ride.

And she told me that same thing in each lesson over the course of days and weeks. I rode Nina, and I rode other horses. Over the course of months, I rode. I even fell off a horse again. Riding is mostly staying on the horse, but a few moments off the horse happen because gravity works.

One Friday night after a particularly long week, I rode Comet. We came around a corner and he tripped, as horses sometimes do. He fell. I fell. I checked on him first, and several others riding in the ring checked on me. We were both fine. I climbed back on him, adjusted my pants that had become pushed into unfortunate areas when I skidded along the shavings, and clucked him into a trot. Halfway down the rail, we approached the corner where we'd both gone ass over teakettle. Fear said hello, and I nodded to her.

And I rode. We both rode for another twenty minutes, and with each gait we did, with each moment, I realized fear slipped away into the confidence that had been brought forth. As I brushed Comet after our ride, one of the younger riders asked me, "Were you afraid when you fell?"

"A little," I said, nudging Comet for his hoof to pick out mud and shavings.

"Do you think he was scared?" she asked, feeding the now wholly not scared Comet a peppermint.

"He might have been."

"But you rode anyway," she declared.

"I rode anyway."

Riding is not as much stellar moments of accomplishments as we strive to perfection as it is steady work, being afraid and riding anyway. Even being afraid and knowing this isn't the right time and horse at the moment and getting off. Riding is not faking courage, but instead allowing enough space for courage and fear to reside together. Fear, after all, is a useful emotion. Just not the only useful emotion. So are confidence, persistence, and belief that day after day, fear does not have the final note in the song of our lives.

Faith is not as much stellar moments of accomplishments as we strive for holy perfection as it is steady work. We listen, we pray, we love. We admit we are afraid to forgive because we were hurt and we might get hurt again. We might be afraid to love because we have lost those we love and grief scares us. We are afraid to ask questions because the answers, if we get them, might lead to more questions. When God meets us in our relationship and says, "Fear not," God isn't telling us to act as if we aren't scared. Instead, God reminds us that fear will not be the only emotion or the conclusive one. When we are scared and fearful, we join a long line of faithful disciples who responded initially with fear, but stayed around.

Faith is being fearful, and fear is part of the life of faith. It is falling off and being bruised and getting back on. Fear is being aware of the risks of love and loving anyway.

If we bring forth the fear within us, we will also find courage. We will also find God.

Vocation

*Discovering vocation does not mean scrambling toward
some prize just beyond my reach but accepting the
treasure of true self I already possess. Vocation does
not come from a voice—out there—calling me to be
something I am not. It comes from a voice—in here—
calling me to be the person I was born to be, to fulfill
the original selfhood given me at birth by God.*

—PARKER PALMER,
LET YOUR LIFE SPEAK[5]

Nina's vocation is a lesson horse. Because of her
lineage, I suspect that is not what her original breeders hoped
for her to be. Her sire and grandsire are champion Saddlebreds.
Nina, for all her gifts, does not have the high-stepping movement
in her trot that performance-level Saddlebreds, those that
compete at the highest level as show horses, have.

I purchased Nina from another barn. She'd had a foal and was then leading a life of meandering around the paddocks, not doing much else. She went from that barn to the barn where I initially began riding, and then, when that barn closed its lesson program, to my current barn.

I'd hoped she could be a lesson horse as well as a horse I could ride regularly, but after our mishap, she got a reputation as too unsteady to use as a lesson horse. I believed my then-instructor. After all, what did I really know about the temperament of horses? And I was still fearful of her—my own horse.

When the first barn ended its lesson program, Nina and I moved to Wingswept, our current barn. While Stephanie, my new (and current) instructor seemed excited about Nina as a horse in the lesson program, I was hesitant.

Imagine my surprise when I arrived at the barn after having ridden there for only a few weeks to see Nina in all her chestnut glory shimmering in the Kentucky summer sun trotting around the outdoor arena with a little person on her. A six-year-old little person, to be exact. Nina looked amazing. She had her head set, a term meaning her head wasn't reaching out or straining against the bridle, but comfortably tucked in near her body. Her neck was stretched long and arched gracefully, a trait Saddlebreds have.

I'd experienced a Nina who was often fussy, who bucked on occasion, and who had very strong opinions about what she wanted to do as a horse. This Nina was a horse I hadn't seen regularly. She was proud and cooperative. She responded to the child's cues and miscues with gentleness.

"That's Nina?" I asked, rather surprised.

"Yes," Stephanie said, not surprised at all.

Some weeks later Nina competed in her first academy show. These shows are the entry-level horse shows. The horses used in these shows are not in regular training as performance show horses and are usually part of a lesson program. I rode her, with modest success. Even more exciting, however, were her rides with small children. Nina, with her height, looks quite striking with small children riding her. She may not be a performance show horse, but she knows when she enters a ring how to show off. Her ears prick forward, her neck stretches to an elegant arch, and her head sets exactly where it should be. And she goes, just as she's supposed to. Walk and trot and canter. Switch directions and do the same. Look like a star, and win a ribbon. She and her riders won several blue ribbons that day, and I was, quite honestly, the proud horse owner.

Nina found her vocation.

She'd actually found it beforehand, but the surroundings were not quite right at our former barn. For reasons known only to Nina, she much prefers her current farm as her home. Horses have quite the communication skill set, and Nina has, almost from day one, communicated her delight at her stall, her community, and her vocation at this new barn.

Vocation has its roots in the late Middle English word that means, "to call." Vocations are our callings, the tasks and jobs in our lives God calls us to do. All Christians are called to the vocation of following Christ. We do that by loving God, loving our neighbor, and loving ourselves.

Too often in the church, vocation is limited to a conversation about whether or not a person has a vocation or call to be ordained while ignoring the fullness of God's call to all of us. Saying vocation is limited to ordained people is as absurd as saying only horses who run in the Kentucky Derby are horses, and the rest are simply lawn ornaments.

Vocation is, for me, the honest involvement in love of God, neighbor, and self lived in the movements of our body and inspiration of our soul. Vocation is not a title or label, but those moments of integrated clarity that we are living God's purpose in what we are thinking, feeling, and doing. A vocation may be a particular profession, like minister or composer, but more often, vocation is expressed in our acts offered in love. We are living our vocation as we till the soil to grow flowers to share with elderly neighbors who live alone. A vocation may be sitting in the hallowed silence of grief with parents who have buried their child. A vocation may be preaching to churches filled with sinners, seekers, and saints or witnessing our experience with the gift of sobriety at an AA meeting.

This honest expression of love isn't so much discovered by tests to uncover our vocation, or committees to discern one, so much as simply by paying attention to the moments when spirit and body intertwine with that mysterious calm and passion of God. Too often, when we lose a sense of vocation, we've lost a sense of ourselves and what brings us fulfillment and joy.

Perhaps we have compared our vocation to someone else's and feel reduced. We get knotted in competitive faith, as if God is ranking our acts of love and only certain vocations matter.

God holds all vocations, all our embodied acts of love, as treasured. God trusts us with this vocation of love. We don't need a certificate to love God, each other, and ourselves. We simply need to remember we are called forth by the voice of God to love. And in this place, we can call each other into the work of love.

Nina does what she does not because she took a quiz or attended a special lesson-horse training school. She simply does it because she found the place she loves, a place that loves her, and a trainer who saw in her what others did not and trusted her to do this job of helping people learn to ride.

Do I wonder what watching her as a fancy show horse would be like? Of course. And if I spent all my time wondering why she isn't a high-stepping show horse, I would miss the love she brings into my life day in and day out in her vocation as Nina.

Nina teaches children and adults to ride. She has more patience than I do on most days with other human beings, and her patience is with new riders being too busy with their reins and pulling on her mouth or too uncertain about what gait they'd like to do. When she's not patient, she expresses that in ways that are clear but still safe for the rider. Nina has taught countless beginning riders to canter. She may not have a fancy trot, but she has a stellar canter. I could canter her and drink a cool glass of sweet tea at the same time.

I don't. But I could and probably never spill a drop.

She has just enough personality to help riders learn to guide and ride, but not so much attitude that she would bolt with a rider. She enjoys thinking there might be a monster in certain corners of the arena, but will respond with a firm seat to go forward, in spite of whatever is lurking in the corners (usually a big pile of nothing). She rolls in fresh shavings with verve and loves to nap in the late afternoons and the late mornings and the late evenings. She is a favorite among many of the young riders, and she is a huge fan of being adored. Her vocation may also be as a princess.

Then again, whose isn't on some days?

Nina holds all that is her vocation as a lesson horse with majesty. She doesn't care what she's not. She lives into what she is. That is vocation.

She would likely be just as happy if her vocation was as a horse of complete leisure, but I know she's a better horse as a busy horse with things to do. Left to her own devices, she thinks napping is her key vocation.

Maybe she's on to something there. I'm fairly certain our communities would be better if we took the vocation of napping as seriously as Nina does.

Nina's whole life—who she is, how she moves, her quirks, and her elegance—is her vocation. She doesn't worry about how she doesn't measure up to other horses, unless the other horses are ponies, and then she expresses her huge displeasure by pinning her ears, a horse's way of saying, "I don't like this, and you're going to hear about it."

Vocation is also knowing what you don't like.

Vocation is a blend of place, person, and gifts strung together by the Holy Spirit. Nina's vocation came about because of what she isn't. She isn't a premier show horse, but she is an amazing lesson horse. She is an amazing lesson horse because my instructor recognized that temperament and movement in her.

Our vocations, our calls from God, work almost the same way. We experiment, perhaps discovering both what we are suited for and even what we are not called to do. We will need insight from others. Usually others can see our vocation before we can. Others can also see what might not be our vocation before we admit we might not be suited for this particular ministry of God.

Vocation is fundamental and basic.

Loving God, each other, and ourselves is deeply simple.

We, of course, make it complicated. I used to lead retreats to help people discover their vocation until one day I wondered aloud, "Why do we think God hides our vocations, our gifts that work to heal the world, in places where only pages of self-assessments and hours-long committee meetings can reveal them?"

God doesn't hide our gifts. They are the very things that are simple, basic, right in front of us. Our vocations are the moments each day when we are present to love. How we do that varies from person to person, but living life as if we must repeat a certain incantation to have our gifts revealed to us misses the point of vocation.

When I watch Nina be who she is, I wonder how many of us avoid our vocation because we spend too much time focused on what we aren't. "I'm not smart enough, rich enough, holy enough, or imaginative enough to do the work of God."

How many of us refuse to hear insight on our vocations from the community in which we live? How many of us fail to see the value of our calls, our gifts, our ministries, because we compare them to others?

Nina lives into her vocation. No, she's not a world champion show horse, not in the way that will put her name in history, but her vocation is valuable, even priceless. She teaches children and adults to love riding. She taught me how to ride her beyond my fear into a love I have for her. She is always the horse I can return to when I need to remember I can ride with confidence.

She preaches, with her life, a flawless sermon on vocation.

Balance

Stir up your power, O Lord, and with great might
come among us; and, because we are sorely hindered
by our sins, let your bountiful grace and mercy speedily
help and deliver us; through Jesus Christ our Lord,
to whom, with you and the Holy Spirit, be honor and
glory, now and for ever. Amen.
—COLLECT FOR THE THIRD SUNDAY OF ADVENT,
The Book of Common Prayer

Stirrups have, in various forms, existed for several thousand years, although the modern incarnation didn't appear until the invention of a saddle with a tree, a stiff core down the middle of the saddle to distribute the pressure and weight of a rider pushing downward in stirrups. No tree means no place for the rider's weight to be carried except on the back of the horse, which makes for an uncomfortable horse and likely a short ride.

In my style of riding, ideally our feet are turned slightly outward—imagine walking on the inside line of your foot—with the ball of your foot on the base of the stirrup and the soles of your boots slightly visible. Toes forward, heels down, knees rolled in, and ride.

Stirrups help with balance. They also help with a myriad of other things like staying in the saddle on a frisky horse and cheating on balance.

Yep, the basic stirrup that helps you ride can also hinder your riding ability. So naturally, riding instructors have developed ways to limit your cheating and develop all the muscles that true balance on a horse requires.

One of these methods is called the two-point stance. If you've watched a horse race, it's the way jockeys ride during the race. The rider stands in stirrups as the horse moves. If you're using the stance to work on balance and leg placement, the rider leans forward with her rear pushing backward. We can use the horse's mane for better balance if needed, but with all your weight essentially in your knees and your feet, it's quite telling how good or poor your balance is.

The first time my instructor explained this to me, I felt quite sure she was joking. Surely this was not something well-balanced people did as they rode?

Well, actually it was something well-balanced people did as they rode . . . to develop and improve balance.

In an early lesson, I asked Stephanie if there was a secret to riding in two-point.

"Doing it."

I roll my eyes regularly during my riding lessons.

And I admit, often months afterward, that my instructor is almost always right.

The first few dozen, maybe hundred times, I tried to ride in two-point stance, I wobbled and fell back into the saddle. I lost my balance and came off the horse a couple of times. I leaned forward too much or not enough. To say my riding was messy and sloppy is an understatement.

Then one day, I felt it. Balance. It was fleeting, but yes, there it was! I'd stood in stirrups, my butt above the saddle, and held on to the horse's mane as she trotted around the arena and done it.

Yay!

Of course, a few moments later, I was off balance again and splatted back in the saddle.

Now, after riding for years, two-point is a stance I can ride in with some competence. The stance itself isn't easy, mainly because it's the physical equivalent of doing four thousand squats on a moving platform, and after a few trips around the arena, my thighs are complaining mightily.

Another sufficient and helpful tool to see how well I am balanced while riding is dropping stirrups completely.

Because why not take away all helps in balance by dropping your irons?

I do it. Riders have what we call No Stirrup November. I had the pleasure of having our summer student instructor at the farm decide I needed to become more aware of my balance and more confident in my balance, so for an entire summer during her lessons, I rode without stirrups. No Stirrup Summer for me.

Any illusions of cheating on balance are dropped when feet slide out of stirrups. Riders find out quickly if we're riding with too much weight in our feet, if we're not stretching our leg downward enough, if our legs are too far forward, or any other things we can do to feel more secure in the saddle than we truly are. When your feet are taken away from you, the knees become very important, as does the seat. Then, of course, you have to pick your irons back up while riding, and this lets you know if your feet are where they should be placed or if you've let them dangle in poor form.

All these drills work on balance, on making me as a rider aware of when I'm balanced and when I'm cheating on my balance, of when my form is helping my balance or hindering my balance, and of how I can continue to strengthen the muscles that assist in my balance.

Balance in riding does not come from one lesson or a dozen lessons. It comes from years of lessons, at least for me. Each horse I ride helps me become more aware of my balance.

Sort of like each person I encounter.

A common theme in the story of humanity and God is that of community. While people do have time away, alone to be present with silence and God, we are mostly with other people. Their quirks, annoyances, gifts, and sins help us check our balance. Are we centered in God, in love, in grace, and the list of all the qualities Jesus asks us to embrace? Or are we putting too much pressure on other things, mainly our own abilities and ideas?

People of faith have spiritual practices, also known as spiritual disciplines, to help with spiritual balance. They include things like fasting, daily prayers, praying with icons, confessing our sins, among a very long list. Like the disciplines that help my balance in riding, spiritual disciplines are activities. They aren't passive ideas that we talk about endlessly. They are faith with work. When I engage in these disciplines, I regularly discover the ways I'm off balance in my practice of the faith Jesus expects from me.

In the Episcopal tradition, Lent, the season before Easter, is a season during which we often add new disciplines to our practice of faith. It's the Christian version of No Stirrup November, when we do some activity to strengthen our faith, and in strengthening that faith, we often realize where we have been deficient, where our perceived balance in God is quite off balance. One Lent, I decided to pray for my enemies, the people in my life who've made me angry, who've dislodged me, and who annoy me.

This discipline first made me admit I actually have enemies. *Enemy* is such a harsh word, I think. But *enemy* is from a root that spans a wide chasm of people, from the Devil, the embodiment of all evil who gets a heap of blame for our very human actions, to someone to whom we are actively or passively hostile. *Enemy* comes from a word that means a person who is literally our un-friend or our not-friend.

Jesus doesn't ask us to love our enemies after he queries us on who has enemies. He knows us too well. We all have enemies, so first and foremost, I had to admit that distasteful truth to myself. I knew people to whom I was actively or, more likely, passively hostile, and who were my un-friends. A quick way to test people from the Deep South on who might be our enemies is an easy one. Do we talk about a person and add, "Bless her heart," at the end of our seemingly overconcerned conversation about her (or his) life events and choices? That's a lovely, passive way to speak of those who are un-friends.

I'm also a priest, and surely priests don't have people in their lives whom they don't like, right? We might think that, but clergy are also human. We are first and foremost human. We are among the people to whom Jesus speaks in the Gospel of Matthew, "You have heard that it was said, 'You shall love your neighbor and hate your enemy.' But I say to you, love your enemies and pray for those who persecute you, so that you may be children of your Father in heaven; for he makes his sun rise on the evil and on the good, and sends rain on the righteous and on the unrighteous."

I so wish at times that the person who wrote the Gospel of Matthew had skipped class that day and missed that lecture from Jesus. I am quite content with praying for those who don't persecute me and who don't annoy me.

The Holy Spirit, as the Spirit is known to do, stirred me upside down and dropped me in the middle of this spiritual discipline. I thought it was good for all of seventeen minutes and five seconds, until I sat down one Ash Wednesday after I'd led church services, calling our congregation to a holy Lent, and began my personal evening prayers. I made a cup of Earl Grey tea and enriched myself with two chocolate-chip cookies, because making a list of people I called *enemy* needed spiritual courage, both from God and chocolate.

I wrote down the first few names, and as I continued to reflect, I felt God pull that stirrup of arrogant assumption from me, that I was in total love and charity with everyone in my life. My balance shifted, and I fell onto the hard ground of reality.

The list was slightly longer than my grocery list for my annual Christmas party, but shorter than the genealogy in First Chronicles, which takes up nine chapters. I counted that a slight win. On any given day, this list includes most politicians, a few bishops, and a lady who lives down the street who lets her smaller-than-a-longhorn cattle (but only slightly smaller) poo in my yard. I've offered her bags, but she tells me it gets in the way of nature.

Over the forty days of Lent, I prayed for these people by name. At first I skipped a few names, especially the names of those who had deeply and personally hurt me. I sat in silence, figuring God knew who I hoped I could pray for. I also wondered if the silence would count as prayer.

God said in some cases, yes, silence was a good prayer, but God wouldn't give me a pass from praying out loud for my enemies. This was quickly becoming the spiritual equivalent of trying two-point stance for the first few times and realizing I was very off balance. I wobbled in the stirrups of faith, and landed hard on my bum after a few fleeting moments.

After thirteen days of sitting in silence with the names of those who must not be named, I decided to speak their first names. My balance strengthened a bit, but I felt every consonant and vowel of these names catch on my soul as I uttered them. Vomit would have been more pleasant.

This was going to be a long forty days. But this was also a discipline, a practice of the balance of my faith. How well could I lift myself up out of the teachings of Christianity I'd interpreted for my own ease and comfort and develop new muscles to balance me in the faith to which Christ called me?

Jesus is not vague about praying for our enemies, and not in a turn-their-hearts, send-a-plague-of-locusts-upon-their-house-and-make-them-agree-with-me kind of way. Jesus wants to turn my heart and help me see them as beloved, wounded children of God. I discovered I was okay with praying for people who didn't agree with me on an intellectual level, such as certain politicians. But when I dropped the stirrups of an intellectual faith and had to sit deeply in my emotions, I realized praying for those who had personally wounded me with their words and deeds was not effortless. Or fun. It didn't even feel edifying.

When I spoke their names aloud in prayer, I remembered what they'd done and how I felt. I fell off my high horse into the muck of the reality of life as humans together. But slowly, excruciatingly slowly, I continued, interspersing my prayers with suggestions to Jesus on how he could make this whole Christian faith much more palatable by omitting this love-your-enemies part.

He did not take my suggestion, but I did feel his. I discovered something in my feelings. My prayers for those who'd hurt me loosened my pain. I began to wonder why these actions wounded me when others' actions didn't, and what I could learn from these wounds. I looked at patterns and habits, and saw forgiveness as less ethereal and more hopeful. The work of checking my balance in faith mattered. I could stand in this place with more strength, not stumbling quite as ungracefully as I had weeks ago. When Easter arrived, I could pray their names.

Unicorns did not dance with rainbows surrounding the earth, and none of the people I prayed for will be invited to dine at my personal table anytime soon, but I will sit with them at God's table.

Praying for my enemies, not just once in a while or even once a week, but daily, gave me more balance in this life of Christlike love. New muscles strengthened me. New awareness expanded me. New practices transformed me.

The Thursday after Easter I was, of course, at the barn. The first of the new foals of the season had been born recently, and I was watching a filly develop her gallop in the paddock. She stood, trotted, and ran with halts and starts, getting ahead and behind herself. Foals have to strengthen their muscles, too, as they learn about this life as a horse. The whole moment reminded me of my disciple of prayer, so I prayed the names of the people for whom I had prayed the previous season.

I prayed them with a balance I hadn't had before, finally standing on my legs in a new way. I discovered that Jesus understood something about the power of praying for those who hurt us, who wounded us, who betrayed us. Praying this way balanced me and healed me.

Praying this way answered my question to Jesus, "Is there a secret to this love-my-enemies thing?"

He rolls his eyes at me and says, "Yes. Doing it."

Routine

*F*or Episcopalians, liturgies in the Book of Common Prayer create the foundation of our worship and express our beliefs. We take much of what is contained between the covers of the Prayer Book, as we call it, for granted. We argue about it, dismiss it, defend it, and, as usual with all things religious, love some of it far beyond reason and detest other parts of it for reasons we will share far beyond a helpful time allocated for discussion.

The Book of Common Prayer was a prophetic step in the liturgies of the church. Its prayers form the services of worship for those gathered in grand cathedrals and small country churches, in their homes for private prayer and in the moments between the great events of life. When the Prayer Book was published for use by the gathering of the faithful, it was the first time the faithful heard the words of the service in the language they spoke regularly. Before the advent of the Prayer Book, services in the Church of England were in Latin, and while more people spoke Latin in 1549 than in the twenty-first century, the number didn't come close to rising to the majority of folks.

The Prayer Book has come down to us in its current incarnation, a mix of deeply ancient and thoroughly modern prayers. We pray them daily, weekly, and seasonally. The cycle of this prayer life is a routine, a liturgy, a work of the people of Jesus.

Liturgy means exactly that, the work of the people. The prayers, silence, and hymns are the work of repetitive devotion.

I've also heard, however, that some people find them boring.

I can understand, even sometimes agree. For Sunday after Sunday during the seemingly endless season after Pentecost in the Episcopal Church, we see the church draped in green vesture, the liturgical color of the season. The blue or purple of Advent is a welcome change when it finally appears. The season after Pentecost extends from the first Sunday after we celebrate Pentecost in early summer, often adorning our churches in the red, orange, yellow, and white colors of holy fire and the Holy Spirit, to the Sunday before the first Sunday of Advent, which begins at the end of November or early in December. We see the color green for a while. A long while.

Then we don't. Suddenly we show up one Sunday to see Advent, with greenery and candles and songs of expectation and waiting. Christmas brings another change; then we move through the seasons of Epiphany, Lent, and the Great Fifty Days of Easter. Before we know it, Pentecost's wild, fierce Spirit blows through the doors and into our lives again, and the calendar starts again.

In this cyclical calendar is the routine of the content of our worship: hymns, prayer, readings from Scripture, the sermon, and the Holy Eucharist. A year in our worship life together will also include baptisms, marriages, and burials. We may celebrate other feasts and fasts that add change and variety, but the routine of our worship is steady.

Steady can feel dull, a sameness of driving on a four-lane highway for thousands of miles through flat grassland with no radio stations to change. Variety is flashy and energetic, inviting us to new and novel experiences. Routine can feel unimaginative, creating space for us to be seduced by something different each moment.

Our faith is grounded, however dull it may seem, by routine.

Routine is the regular workout at the gym, week after week, to care for our bodies. Routine is the comfort when the changes and chances that burst into our lives leave us longing for the days with expected moments and hours. Routine steadies us, strengthens us, nourishes us.

Routine is praying daily, even when the prayers feel dry and empty. Routine is riding lessons each week, practicing the same gaits, working on undoing some of the same bad habits, and cleaning the same saddle with the same saddle soap.

I explained this to a friend visiting from out of town. She wanted to ride horses. I'm always happy to comply.

"So, what do you do when you ride?"

I explained that we arrive at the barn and we brush the horse. Then we tack up the horse. After that preparation is complete, we ride, working on the walk, trot, and canter, both rider position and horse position. After we are done, we untack the horse, put everything away, and groom the horse one final time.

"Oh." Her response indicated she had images of us climbing in the saddle and chasing down wild buffalo.

Nevertheless, we went and we rode.

After the lesson, she asked, "So you do that every time?"

"Yep, with occasional variation that may or may not be good, depending on how willing I was to listen to my horse," I replied. "But, yes, I do that every time."

Every time, I bridle a horse. Every time, I pay attention to keeping my toes forward and my heels down. Every time, I work on the position of my shoulders, especially keeping them open. Every time, I think about sitting deeply in the saddle and calling for the gaits clearly. Every time, I brush the horse. Every time. I lean my forehead against the warmth of one of these stunning creatures and breathe in the magic smell.

Every time.

Riding is an enormous amount of practice and routine. Even when I walk the horse, I'm working on my leg position. Is the line from my shoulders to my hips to my heels a straight one? Are my knees turned inward? Are my toes forward? Are my hands quiet? Am I listening to the horse?

Riding is an enormous amount of muscle memory, both physical muscles and soul muscles. Calf muscles learn how to push downward and outward. Hips feel stronger rolled down and in, and the core feels confident sitting up instead of leaning forward.

Your physical muscles do not learn those positions from one lesson or ten lessons. They learn from every lesson. Yes, after years of riding saddle seat my body knows what to do, mostly. I self-correct in ways I didn't two years ago, and I make some of the same mistakes I made years ago.

Soul muscle memory plays a role in riding, too. Confidence has to sit in the saddle with my seat. Horses are profoundly aware of emotions in the saddle. When I'm unsure and fearful, horses may decide there is something out there they, too, should be afraid of, or they may decide this rider isn't going to make them do anything, so let's have fun—as the horse defines fun, which may or, more often, may not be fun for the rider.

That memory is more difficult for me. My soul remembers much more slowly than my muscles do in the saddle. For the first few moments on a horse, I take three deep breaths, and with each exhale I release anxiety, perfectionism, and the fear I don't need.

Hey, we do what works to keep us in the saddle.

Routine can also feel so comfortable that we never reach into variety. Lucky for me my riding instructor ensures that I don't get too comfortable with routine horses. One night, I arrived at the barn on a surprisingly warm winter evening to discover I was riding Izzy.

Izzy and I have a challenging relationship, but our disagreement is not her fault. She is an opinionated horse with quirks and eccentricities that I bring out in her at a stellar level. She likes steady contact with her reins, especially in the corners. I get anxious and have busy, fussy hands. She doesn't like my calves too close to her body, and when I sense her getting fussy, I can wrap my calves along her sides.

She's opinionated about how she holds her head and enjoys getting in the head of her riders. She's quick to decide whether or not she respects whoever is on her back, and if she decides she doesn't respect you, the ride will be a short one filled with unpleasantness.

I've had several short rides on Izzy.

I've also had several long rides on other horses, and I've settled into the routine with my hands and calves and seat. So up I went, and into my head Izzy went.

Our first few passes at the trot weren't bad, although holding my breath makes riding rather difficult. I eventually realized I needed to breathe while riding, as passing out from lack of oxygen wouldn't help Izzy respect me at all. I also realized something else. All my many routine rides where I worked on shoulder position and heel position and every other body part position mattered.

I noticed Izzy listened to me as we trotted the straightaways. She tested me in the corners, but Steph yelled, "Bottom rein!" and I knew, from many routine rides, how gently to take up on the bottom rein to balance her as we went into the corners. My body knew how to lower my post, not going so high in the saddle, to slow my body and, in turn, slow her trot.

Steph, ever the genius instructor, had me ride the horse. I had the least confidence in riding in a crowded arena, directing me to concentrate on several other young riders who were novice riders and one other rider on a horse who enjoys kicking other horses. "Concentrate on them, not the horse you're on." Those many riding lessons helped me trust my body, trust the feel, and allow my vision to see the arena.

Trust all those routine lessons, and quit overthinking. Ride from routine.

At the end of our quite uneventful, surprisingly routine ride, Izzy and I parted as friends. Even our first canter start, which had the makings of a disaster, smoothed out into a lovely gait. I did quit while I was ahead, ending on a good note.

Another lesson learned from routine: End with a win. When it's all gone well, pet the horse, love on her, and end as friends.

Izzy, of course, doesn't really like anyone touching her neck, so I scratched her ears, which had spent many moments during our ride pinned against her head in that "Hey, I'm thinking about doing something naughty" way horses do, and kissed her nose. She will always challenge me as a rider. She will always make me want to have a drink before I get on her (I don't, but I think about it). And she will always remind me of the deep and simple grace of practice and of routine in my riding life and in my spiritual life.

Collect

This morning I turned my coffeemaker on. I'm not a morning person, so pushing a button is the limit of my fine motor skills in the minutes after I first rouse myself from sleep. My coffeemaker is one of those nifty horrible-for-the-environment-but-excellent-for-my-morning-haze machines where I can drop in a pod, press a button, and magically coffee fills my cup while I'm barely awake.

Except for this morning, when I pressed the button of magic glory and the coffee spilled forth . . . onto the counter.

My brain was unwilling to process quickly why the brown liquid of life was pooling on the counter and now dripping onto the floor.

Oh, the cup, my sluggish brain reflected as I looked in my hand at the empty cup I still held. I shoved the cup underneath the stream of coffee, sighed deeply, and burst into tears.

Granted, crying over spilled coffee is an acceptable response. It is, after all, the magical elixir of hope and joy. But this response was a sign of something deeper.

I needed to collect myself.

As I wiped up the coffee and made a new cup, I slid down my kitchen door until I sat on the floor. Holding my coffee and propping my arms on my knees, I felt sprawled across miles, parts of me sloppy and spilled over life at the moment. Too many people, moments, ideas, and issues pulling my head forward and down. Too many times of hearing my name followed by, "Can I ask you a question?" taking my energy. Too many emails and text messages that keep my feet stuck in mud, limiting my forward movement into a day off and time away from work. I am at the same time racing to meet the demands I put on myself and others place on my life and incapacitated by the cement around the expectations of these same demands. I feel scattered and unbalanced, too much of me pulled forward by the expectations of others and too little of my own energy grounding me to God.

I carry a deep, buried need to be loved and to be useful to people in my life, likely because I carry wounds connecting my value solely to how others value me. When I decide I'm the only person who reaches for external validation, my therapist reminds me this is common among human beings. We, quite basically, love to be loved and love to be needed. If we aren't attuned to these needs, and even if we are, we too often find ourselves saying yes to every request, being available to everyone who has a need, and giving our time and energy to everyone who asks us to place more of ourselves on the altar. It's one reason I think most humans who have lived this life and have the scars to prove it will benefit from therapy, a support group, or active spiritual direction at some points along our life journey.

We humans have issues.

We will, by our vocation of being people of faith, have traumatic, heartbreaking moments and be present with other people on their journeys through these moments. No one gets to journey through life without walking through the valley of the shadow of death, and we will fear as we walk, regardless of the poetry of the twenty-third psalm.

I've been with people through the call from the doctor with the worst possible news, with those who made their own funeral plans before turning off the life support, and with the staggeringly difficult times of the awareness of the devastation of addiction in their lives. I've heard crises of faith, crises of life and love, and the paralyzing uncertainty that is present to all humans in life.

And we are expected to offer something in these cataclysmic moments.

In our best moments, we extend an affirming comfort that grief, sadness, and despair are part of the natural course of being human. We sit with, hold space, and offer presence.

Then we replenish ourselves. We, like Jesus, move away from the crowd and take time alone. We take our days off and our vacation and our retreats.

Or we don't. I am an overfunctioner. And I had not pushed away the 1,200-pound creature that was my overfunctioning self, trying desperately to meet everyone's needs and wants, when it claimed my personal space.

So now I was underfunctioning with spilled coffee and tears on a Saturday morning. Sitting on the floor an hour before I was planning to go to the horse barn in the middle of a full-on ugly cry complete with snot and stuttering breathing is perhaps not the ideal way to begin one's morning. But it was the most honest way for me.

I felt overrun and possessed by the expectations of others and by the part of my soul that realized I'd decided to do everything and anything that needed to be done, including checking on a neighbor who had recently been widowed, filling holes in the church grounds dug by industrious moles, and accepting the emotional baggage of a good friend whose ex-husband married an Episcopalian and it was somehow my fault. My inner first grader picked up her purple crayon and circled the two that did not belong on my to-do list.

"I cannot do everything," I confessed, then followed with a bare whisper. "But they will be angry at me."

I wasn't certain who the magical *they* were. Gnomes, perhaps, who lived in my garden? Real people who answered polls from God about how well I was living this Christian life?

On a scale from one to five, five being the highest, how well has Laurie met your expectations of Christlike love?

"Probably," the part of me that pushed back against horses who didn't honor my boundaries replied. Horses do that. Just like humans. They will shove against a person standing near them to see what they do. If you move, they push some more.

If you push back, they realize the boundary.

I had been pushed by expectations and had not pushed back. Now all these expectations pushed me straight down on the floor.

My inner self continued, "They will keep pushing, taking as much of your soul as you offer. All of it, if you let them. Do you really want to spend the rest of your days sitting on the floor with coffee dripping on you?"

At this very moment, sitting on the kitchen floor with my cup of coffee is the only thing I want to do.

She, however, had other ideas. She, this same part of me that shoves 1,200-pound horses around to claim her personal space, reminds me that the commandment to love God and love our neighbor also commands me to love myself. She also reminds me that a horse is waiting for me at the barn.

Loving myself sometimes means disappointing others. She, this holy part of me, reminds me of this deep truth. She swears. She is not afraid of anger, mine or yours. She does not give me so freely to those who consume me. She's very good at collecting the rest of me back into myself. She's very good at reminding me what needs to be done.

I simply have to remember her voice, the one that reminds me what needs to be done and what does not need to be done and the boundary between the two.

This part of me also remembers I am responsible for centering my energy back into God and for finding the direction to which God is guiding me, not the direction others are pulling me. Because others will pull at me. We pull at each other. We humans will take from each other as we can, like a giant buffet of soul energy. We will sprawl and grasp and move ourselves in every direction but the one in which God really would like us to move.

Oh yes, I need to collect myself.

Or, more correctly, I need to allow God to collect me. I need God to remind me to take time and find the parts of myself and soul that have been stretched too far by demands and expectations, both mine and others, and bring them back to center. I need God to pull my intellect and heart closer together, to connect them, so I could move through this muck that was currently stagnating me.

So, I get off the floor and go to the barn.

Collect.

Collecting a horse refers to focusing the horse, centering her, gathering her energy for the benefit of both rider and horse. A collected horse takes shorter steps rather than long, extended ones. The horse's weight is in the back end of the horse, so the front part of the horse is lifted. Horses move from their back end, pushing forward, and collecting maximizes that movement. Collecting a horse also involves impulsion, the forward-moving energy. Impulsion is not racing at a high speed, but instead finding a pace at which a horse looks best moving forward with energy and collection. Collected horses have an upward movement to their gaits instead of exclusively forward movement.

During a lesson my instructor asked me to collect my horse. I looked at her as if she'd also asked me to sprout wings and fly. She explained, "Imagine shortening the space between the horse's head and her tail and moving her up and forward in that smaller space."

Oh, that.

Instead of letting a horse's energy sprawl forward and amble backward, the rider who collects a horse uses leg pressure to drive a horse forward while keeping the horse's weight slightly more in the hind legs. A rider's hands hold steady and gently work the bit back and forth to coax the horse's head back and up, if needed. Horses, like humans, slump when they are tired or lazy, so they can drop their heads instead of carrying them higher and upward. A collected horse's energy and movement becomes focused and directed. This only happens, however, if the rider is as focused and directed.

When I first started riding at my current barn, Stephanie would give me step-by-step instructions on collecting a horse: lift your hands, shorten your reins, sit back, move her bit right and left to get her attention, touch her sides with your calves to move her forward, sit deep, and cluck. Clucking is a sound riders make, along with saying the actual words like *trot* or *canter* to cue the horse. As I gained more riding experience and became more aware of the value of collecting a horse, Stephanie began to simply yell, "Collect!" and many parts of my body and mind would respond to her as the horse responds to me.

The descriptive words of this sound easier than the act of collecting is, at least to me. Keeping a horse moving forward in the gait while working her weight back and her head up is somewhat counterintuitive. Therefore, I need my legs to push forward and a sense of balance in my seat to use my back end to help the horse use her back end.

Collecting a horse is a routine part of riding, and it's a constant process of learning. I collect better than I did several years ago, and I'm still learning how to use all these aids—my hands, my legs, my voice, my seat, my mind, and my instinct—to collect better each time I ride. When I'm on a horse who's riding a bit loose and often too fast to look her best, I need to collect myself first to collect her. I sit balanced. I use gentle but firm hands to work her head and front end back and slightly up, pushing her forward with my legs to keep her going somewhere, all while staying on this moving creature.

Collecting a horse is, in part, finding the balance between control, energy, and direction—the rider's and the horse's. Enough movement of the reins and bit to guide the horse's head, enough pressure of the leg to propel the horse forward, enough space for the horse to move, and enough balance of the rider to sit back and deep all combine for the horse and rider to find a direction, make a plan, and go somewhere.

You can see why collecting is a dance of opposites as we find the pace we need, the energy we need, and the balance we need.

In horses and in humans.

Collect.

In the Book of Common Prayer, and in the ancient Christian tradition of worship, there is the collect, a particular prayer type. The collect is among the opening prayers of the Holy Eucharist and in the final prayers of the Daily Office, the prayers we pray in morning and evening. They are said at the beginning of the Holy Eucharist, collecting the people in prayer and worship—hence their name, we think, although the original meaning is lost to us. Sometimes they reflect the themes of the readings from the Bible that day. Other times they simply remind us how God gathers us to strive to love, to confess our sins, to stir up the yearning for God's justice and mercy for all humanity. Their poetry in prayer has been forming for more than a thousand years, keeping our movement forward into modernity while pulling us ever so slightly back in tradition so our collective movement in worship in prayer is held together by the bridle of God's love for humanity.

Derek Olsen explains their importance in worship, describing collects as "bite-sized crystallizations of doctrine, interpretation, and practice . . . a primary source of our theology. Repeating them day after day, week after week, year after year, instills a shared theological vocabulary within the praying community."[6]

When we come to worship in our communities, we arrive in our various states of disorganization and disarray. We live our lives in these same states. In our spiritual states, we imagine the saints as centered, focused women and men of God who are as steady in their faith as a bass line, the deep thrum of music that never shifts or moves too much from center.

Our reality, and the reality of many of the saints, is that we are harried and unsettled, parenting our faith like a two-year-old who has had no sleep and too much sugar. Our shoes don't match our outfit. We aren't sure our underwear is even on right-side outward. Our outfits are coordinated only by the spit-up on each piece. We fly into worship late, hope there's a place in the back pew, see there isn't, and slink to the front, not sure what's going on and feeling lost in all the other people settled into prayer, or at least we think they are settled.

I'm sure people look at me, standing at the altar, wearing vestments, holding my hands in the orans position as I lead prayer. I suppose I look collected.

Some Sundays I'm feeling all kinds of collected and living at the speed best to show my soul to the world. The pace of the prayers is consistent. I feel my feet standing deeply connected to the ground, rooted in faith and grace. The touch of God's hands on me has balanced me. The exuberance of faith is palpable. And I'm having a good hair day.

But honestly, most Sundays, the weight of the expectations has me off balance. I'm shifting as I lead the prayers, wondering if I'm praying the words well enough, like my seminary professors taught me. Am I rushing? Did I sing the part okay, or was my voice too shaky? Dammit, I forgot to mention the announcement about the soup we need for our food bank. And my sermon . . . ugh.

I may not be on the floor with coffee spilling everywhere, but my own overly functioning sense of perfection means God gets to collect me even in the moments I look most collected. This morning, after I got myself off the floor and cleaned up the coffee and, to some extent, myself, I went to the barn.

Some days are like that for me. I don't feel collected at all, but life is waiting. So, God shifts my soul back and forth to get my attention focused. On certain days, God collects me to the speed I need to move, remembering what tasks of love are mine and what works of love belong to someone else. Some days God realizes I need to collect myself in a deeply internal way, stilling my soul in silence and calm. I may do that by watching Netflix all day or spending time in prayer at the barn.

I pray well at the barn. The acts of brushing a horse and preparing her and me for a ride give ample time to pray. On this day, God uses an imperceptible moment to collect me. I climb into my saddle and gather Nina's reins. The tips of my fingers of my left hand graze the edge of Nina's snaffle rein and its leather braid, slightly sticky from saddle soap. I usually have my gloves on when I ride, but in the midst of today's coffee disaster and subsequent cry-fest, I'd forgotten them, so my bare fingers encounter this texture and stay in the moment.

Nina, feeling my touch through the rein, moves her head to the left slightly, then nods, as if to urge me on from the barn to the arena. This touch and Nina's movement draw my awareness into this space, a tactile nudge from the Holy Spirit to settle.

The holy space of the barn is filled with its prayers this morning. The sounds of tack being brought to various stalls, the movement of the horses as they eat hay, and the gait calls and clucks from riders in the arena. I feel God collect me with these prayers. Their familiar cadence settles me into myself a bit more, keeping my weight into the ground and lifting up my gaze to see even just a bit beyond what is distracting me or concerning me at the moment to allow grace to enter my field of vision. God guides me to the pace that is best for me this day.

I would like to say the routine of riding fully collects me every day. It doesn't. Some days I'm fully present to the time with God and horses, offering presence and prayers as I ride after a day that demands God, horses, and prayers. Other times my attention is drawn from the profound moment of prayer and horses to a fly annoying both me and the horse. I've felt God's legs push me forward from any number of things I need to leave behind, and I stubbornly turn in a circle and refuse to move forward.

Even in these places, God collects me. Gently in the beginning, a slight shift in my soul reminding me to lean back in prayer, whether it's a traditional prayer in a traditional place like a church, or on a trail ride where the two or three that are gathered in Jesus's name include a rider, a horse, and a dog. Maybe I remember a prayer I've memorized. Maybe my prayer is something raw, something along the lines of "Lord, I'm here. That's the best I've got today," if I can even manage complete sentences. Maybe it's a string of profanity. I've been known to pray those not-safe-for-work prayers.

God settles me back into the foundation of myself, reminding me I will disappoint others and even myself, and I will still be loved by God. I feel God working me back into myself when I've gotten too extended and too stretched because I am tired or irritated, giving me courage to claim holy space for me, even when that holy space is a marathon of Gilmore Girls. God sits deeply on me to slow me down so I can live at the speed best for me at the moment. God directs me to the truth that those who love me don't need an explanation to my "No," and those who don't love me won't believe my explanation, anyway.

God collects me, directs me, and sends me back into myself, the me who prays and pushes a horse and the person who is invading my space when needed, the me who can be present with the pain and distress of others, not to heal them, but instead to sit with them and help when appropriate and, most importantly, when asked. God collects me when my life is in disarray, when my thoughts are too far out in front of my life, my energy disgorged in ways that drain me. As I find myself sitting on the floor, clutching a cup of coffee and wiping my tears and snot on a rag that had previously been used to mop up coffee, God collects me with words of prayer, with silence, with tears, and with anger.

God collects me, pulling the bit of my soul to gently raise my head to see another point of view, shifting my energy from pulling forward to sitting back, allowing my movement to come from my foundation, my seat of the soul.

God collects me back into myself.

Blame

Those who blame the horse will go through a lot of
horses looking for the one that is perfect.
—SMITH LILLY,
SADDLE SEAT HORSEMANSHIP[6]

One of the early lessons in riding I learned: It's not the horse's fault.

Blaming the horse is an easy option when, for the 329th time, I've tried to call for the canter and gotten the incorrect lead, or tried to trot a horse forward who instead backs around in circles. Blaming the horse is easy when she's trotting around the arena uncollected and too fast. Blaming the horse is easy when I look sloppy in the saddle.

Blaming the horse is easy when my rides are not going as expected because the horse cannot, in a traditional verbal way, stop and say, "What? You're the idiot who keeps calling for the canter with your reins too tight."

They communicate their displeasure with my riding quirks, usually by not doing what I want them to do. Blaming the horse may be easy, but it isn't helpful. Horses almost always are responding to our cues. When Nina is picking up her canter on the wrong lead, sure, she may simply be selling me out because she can, but she more likely is doing so because I'm not cueing her strongly enough while giving her the space to sell me out.

Blaming the horse diverts my responsibility as a rider. After all, for as amazing and wise as horses are, we humans have a few skills on them. We have opposable thumbs, for one. Horses can learn by watching and doing repeatedly, as can humans, but we humans can learn by our own reflection and contemplation. Hopefully, although I'm becoming more and more convinced this ability does not extend to all humans.

Blame covers the mirror of reflection so we can't see ourselves. Instead, we project onto others. Maybe blame is a default human ability that entered our skill set when we recognized the difference between good and evil. Eve and Adam, when asked by God, "Who told you that you were naked? Did you eat from the fruit of the tree I told you not to eat from?" respond with blame. Adam blames Eve and God, after all, saying, "*You*, God, gave her to me." Eve blames the serpent, saying, "He tricked me!" instead of, "Well, you know, I got some information that may or may not have been complete and acted on it impulsively." We never hear from the serpent before God lays down the new law on him.

Disobedience and lack of trust in God may have been the initial sins, but blame showed up at the party soon afterward. I have always wondered what would have happened if Eve and

Adam had taken responsibility for their actions. Might we have gotten the Garden of Eden on alternate weekends instead of being banished forever?

We didn't. Instead we blame horses for not trotting the way we'd like them to trot; our economic situation on "those people," whoever they may be; our personal disappointments on events of our past or the dashed expectations of the present. We blame everyone else, and forget to look at ourselves.

We forget to look at the reflection of ourselves in other people.

Riding has clarified this reflection for me. Horses do almost exactly what we ask them to do. They are a reflection of us. If I'm having a ride where Nina is not responding to me as I'd like her to respond, I have to remember I'm the rider. I love that Nina has her bitchy horse moments, because I have learned not to get frustrated and blame her, but to be clearer and more firm in my riding. She may have her days when her attitude flows from her mane and tail, but when I keep asking her, not blaming her, but asking her to respond to me, she does. And she looks quite fancy doing so.

I recall the times of hearing my instructor ask me, in her rhetorical style, "Did you give her permission to trot, or did you call for the canter?" and my lame reply, "But Nina"—or whatever the name of the horse I was riding—"isn't doing this right."

The first few times I replied with that, Steph would coach me, correcting me to the cues I needed to communicate.

Then one day, before I even got the words of blame out, she said, "It's not the horse's fault."

I'd like to say she never had to say that to me again. She did, but I haven't heard her say it to me in a long while. Because somewhere in the regular rides and the instruction and frustration and success, I realized blaming the horse prevented me from improving as a rider. Instead, I needed to be willing to recognize what I was doing wrong as a rider and how I can do whatever I need to be doing differently. I needed to reflect.

Don't get me wrong, the reflection is still staring into a mirror dimly. As with Eve and Adam, blame seems to be a default vocabulary for me. After all, blaming others is so much easier than self-reflection and responsibility. I have a gift for seeing the faults of others so very clearly, particularly when their thoughts, words, and deeds have not met my expectations.

Seeing those same things in myself?

Not so much. My interactions with other humans suggests to me Eve and Adam's infatuation with blame is alive and well in humanity's DNA.

My horse, my shockingly honest friends, and my therapist have helped, but I will always be grabbing the mirror cleaner to wipe off the layers of dust and dirt to help my vision see myself clearly and unflinchingly. Our faith that God loves us, the wonderful parts and the seedy, damaged parts, invites us to have the courage to see the fullness of ourselves and our souls and identify the parts that may need God's hand in healing and transformation.

Too often, however, we get entwined in a moral judgment about our not-so-shiny aspects, and we keep them buried in the back closets of the basements of our consciousness. We lose sight of the faith that God loves us, all of us, and become fearful that if we admit the existence of our default tendency to blame, to hold others to unreasonable standards of behavior, to ignore boundaries, or whatever actions we embody that twist and distort love, God will not love us.

One thing helpful with blame and horses is a lack of moral consequence. My riding skills or lack of them are not mortal or venial sins. If I admit my fault, doing so is not a condemnation on my mortal soul. Instead, it is a reminder to own my mistakes and rectify them through learning. The move from blame to responsibility is one that improves my riding.

Admitting our fault in our human relationships feels much more consequential. Blame builds walls around us after the initial hurt or disappointment. These walls—we might even call them boundaries—give us safe space. Responsibility helps us decide if those boundaries need to remain firmly in place, be more malleable, or eventually be demolished.

Make no mistake, we are victimized by others, and in turn we victimize others. We are victimized by a culture that denies the dignity of our gender, our race, our ethnicity, our sexuality, our economic situation, or a long list of qualities. Some of these sins are so wounding, so serious, that blame is wholly appropriate, and we are in no way responsible for the damage done to us. Victims of sexual abuse and violence do not ask for this and are not to blame. Blaming people for their own poverty, for their own victimization by a system that abuses, for being victims of war—those are reflections of our own twisted blame. We are abdicating our responsibility for them. We as Christians do not get the pass of seeing our sisters and brothers crushed by poverty, sickness, and hate and shrugging our shoulders. We may not have caused their harm, but we are responsible for undoing the harm and being a presence of healing.

What we do with our blame can be holy or harmful. God does that, gives us a choice. Do we want to ingest the role of powerless casualty of someone else's choices, or do we want to trust in the transformation of responsibility? Do we want to stay where we are or do we want to learn? Do we want to repeat the mantra, "It's his/her/their fault," until we fully believe it, or will we eventually allow that mantra to shift into, "Hmmm, I wonder what I can learn from this pain?" Do we want to act as if all the hate and harm in the world magically appeared while we were reading the Bible, so we can blame someone else? Or do we want to live up to our promise to love our neighbors as ourselves and be responsible for healing the world?

Humans seem to find blame as the gateway to the garden of blissful unawareness, as if wandering naked from any responsibility, any choice or control, is the preferred state of being for us as God's beloved creations. When we are cast out from this false garden into the world, we have work to do.

When Eve and Adam got sent packing from the Garden, their consequences included work, toil, and labor outside the Garden. Shifting from blame to responsibility and transformation takes work. I wish it didn't. I wish we could lounge in the comfort of blame while ordering fruity, slushy drinks from cabana boys as we float in bliss. But we don't. We get to work. Blame means, at some level, we don't have to acknowledge the brokenness, disappointments, damaging lessons learned, grief, and denial of our dignity by others and ourselves in our lives, or we don't have to acknowledge our own role in the brokenness, grief, and denial of dignity in others.

No horsewoman or man will find the perfect horse. We can find horses that work particularly well with our strengths in riding who build our confidence when we ride their exuberant trots around the arena. We will also find horses whose personalities and quirks will invite us to blame them for their fabulous ability to show us the areas of our riding that need improvement and work. My experience as a rider is these horses transform me as a rider when I move past blame and take responsibility for listening to the riding lessons they share with me when I get into the saddle.

No person will ever find the perfect friend, partner, horse, job, faith community, or any of the external things we so want to layer around us to shore up our internal shortcomings. We will find those people and communities that build our confidence and sustain us in times of our own weakness. More importantly, these same people and communities will also challenge us. God invites us to pay attention to these moments, as they are offering us the holy lesson of responsibility and transformation.

Responsibility is the holy transformation of blame. We step up. We acknowledge. We, despite and even because of our own wounds, get busy with the faithful work of healing, of helping, of doing more than wishing things would get fixed. Responsibility empowers us. We stop looking for the perfect partner, the perfect job, the perfect horse, or the perfect faith community, and we start remembering the capabilities and responsibilities God has given us and get to work honing them and developing them.

We respond to God's asking us to love and serve. The hate and brokenness may not be our fault (although many times it is), but responding to it is most certainly our responsibility.

Deep

Riding is, in many ways, done through your seat, your backside; that part of our anatomy about which so many women feel less than enthusiastic is the very thing critical to riding. Riding circles call it an independent seat, the ability to sit deeply balanced in the saddle while freeing your hands, arms, shoulders, thighs, knees, calves, and feet to move and aid as needed. How horses can feel slight shifts in weight and pressure from my backside through a leather saddle to their soul is something just south of magical.

And yet they can.

A rider's seat is the foundation for communicating to a horse.

Not that I fully believed, at first, how the shift of hips and drop of my backside deeply into the saddle would really matter that much. Several times in my early riding (and a few times even now), when the horse I'm riding is a bit more energetic and out of control than he needs to be, I heard, "Sit deep!" from Steph, yelled at me from across the arena.

Imagine sitting, letting gravity and weight work with you. Even though in this current position, we think we are sitting deeply, most of us aren't. We're pulled up slightly, probably even leaning forward. When we flatten our spine somewhat with our core muscles, knit our ribs together, and let the bones, muscles, and fat that is our backside drop, even push down slightly into our seat—that is sitting deeply.

Sitting deeply allows our buttocks to take the weight of our feet. Scientists observe that one of the purposes of our oft-maligned parts of anatomy is to allow primates to rest without placing all the weight on our feet. In riding, sitting deeply is a purposeful move that does exactly that. Our body weight shifts from our feet in the stirrups to our weight in our butt sitting in the saddle. This shift gives better balance. When I am sitting deeply with an active core, the rest of my body is relaxed, fluid, and useful as I communicate with my horse.

This body position grabs the soil of creation, reaching downward into the earth. And yet it allows the hips and pelvis to move freely and follow the motion of the horse. Sitting deeply is at the same time fixed and flexible. The position stretches downward to the horse and upward through the crown of our heads. It is a perfect meditation position, as long as you find meditating on the back of an almost-galloping, 1,200-pound creature of God calming.

I happen to find doing so calming in that sure, this-could-escalate-very-quickly-into-a-terrifying-moment way. And yet, as I sit deeply, riding a canter is profoundly calming. Horses sense this seat as a kind of a brake. The deeper a rider sits, the more collected and often slower a horse goes in his gait. Riding a canter is, in its essence, the art of sitting deeply on a horse that is going forward in a very controlled gallop.

As is often true with horses and faith, things that seem to live on the extreme ends away from each other are held together quite elegantly.

Notice the riders at the Kentucky Derby. They aren't sitting on the horses. They are hovering above them, balancing in two-point position to allow the horses to run as fast as possible. Their balance is in their knees and core.

Speed is useful, needed, and necessary in racing and in living life. We may find ourselves in dangerous places, uncomfortable situations, and we need to get out, quickly.

But speed is not sustainable. Horses and humans can only run at top speed for so long. We can only lean in and balance as we flee from life for a limited amount of time until our physical selves collapse.

What is sustainable?

Sitting deeply. Dropping the weight into the parts of our incarnate selves that were formed by God to take the whole weight of our selves. Pushing downward through muscle, fat, and bones to anchor our souls to the soul of the horse.

Tally is a lesson barn favorite because she is a retired show horse. She has finesse and energy. Her trot is energetic and her canter, if collected, is so smooth that you can sit deeply and ride her canter while fishing around in your jacket for a tissue, find said tissue, blow your nose because it's cold season in Kentucky, and replace the tissue in your pocket and never miss a beat. I speak from experience on that one.

Notice, I said *if* she's collected.

Tally is a retired show horse, and all that energy is more than happy to dash around the arena if her rider has loose reins and isn't sitting deeply. I know this from experience, as well. Tally was dashing around the arena with me one afternoon. After a couple of years of lessons and my hearing, "Sit deep!" 823 times or so and still not sitting deeply, I was having a moment.

In the past, to slow her down I fiddled with her reins, which didn't work. I pushed out my feet, which didn't work. I rolled my shoulders back, to no avail.

And then I sat deep. I rolled my hips under and rolled my knees inward and felt my pelvis drop. It's a small movement, probably almost imperceptible to someone watching me dash around on Tally from the viewing stands.

She slowed and collected. With just that small movement. She felt it and, more importantly, she responded to it. Tally and I had communicated. I'd made a request, and she honored it.

Sit deep.

One of my favorite books in the Hebrew Bible is Jonah. It has significant scenes with the main named character sitting deep. Jonah tries everything he can to flee from God, dropping deeply into the nave of a ship, dropping deeply into a sleep as a storm rages, threatening to sink the ship, asking the pagan sailors to drop him into the great deep where he promptly gets swallowed by a great fish and sits deeply within the belly of the fish. He gets vomited by the fish, where he sits deeply in fish vomit and gets a great do-over in life.

We initially meet Jonah when God asks him to get up, go, and proclaim to Nineveh. Jonah does the exact opposite. Yet after Jonah gets up and goes to do the exact opposite of what God has asked, we meet Jonah again, sitting deeply in fish vomit when God asks him again to get up, go, and proclaim to Nineveh. Jonah complies, meeting the letter of the words of God's request more than the spirit of God's request, I suspect. And at the end of the book, we hear Jonah has succeeded wildly. The people of Nineveh have repented, and the cattle have repented. Jonah is a successful prophet, almost an oxymoron in biblical literature.

Yet we find Jonah at the end of the text sitting deeply with his own anger. He's frustrated, to put it mildly.

The book of Jonah shares this scene: "But this was very displeasing to Jonah, and he became angry. He prayed to the Lord and said, 'O Lord! Is not this what I said while I was still in my own country? That is why I fled to Tarshish at the beginning; for I knew that you are a gracious God and merciful, slow to anger, and abounding in steadfast love, and ready to relent from punishing. And now, O Lord, please take my life from me, for it is better for me to die than to live.'"

Jonah is angry that God is kind and loving, not just in word, but in deed. Jonah has touched and encountered God's kindness, not just preached about it. And he is so angry that he just wants to die.

That's angry.

I appreciate Jonah's model of sitting deeply in his anger. Too often the spiritual model is sitting deeply with calm, focus, and peace. Maybe that's the ideal, like riding with an independent deep seat, but for many of us, the minute we slow down and try to sit deeply, we're assaulted with the emotions that we've been running from for a while, those less-than-charming emotions of anger, rage, frustration, envy, pride, and the like. The emotions that don't make our list of qualities we'd share with a potential employer or with God.

Far too many of us have heard from the institutional church and her spokespeople how these feelings are sinful, how we should be ashamed of experiencing them, and how the only time they should be spoken aloud is during a time of confession.

I've heard how distasteful anger is supposed to be in women. "No one likes an angry woman," my grandmother would say when I'd express my anger over behavior that, after years of therapy, I realized fully deserved anger as an appropriate response.

Our ancestors in the faith thought the story of Jonah and his sitting deeply in anger was an important story, perhaps because we don't see God absent from Jonah in this place, but instead we see God with Jonah in this place.

Jonah is sitting in his anger, which at best is bordering on self-involved, and God is sitting right next to him. God is not afraid to sit with our authentic feelings. God is not condemning of our feelings. God does not ignore or deny our feelings.

God does suggest that we consider what we do with our feelings.

Sitting deeply is not my default nature. My intimate relationship with anxiety has forced me to develop some methods to reach this state. Taking deep breaths when I get on the horse, giving space for my anxiety when I ride a new horse, and mentally sending my anxiety into my core where I can capture it in a way with my muscles all help at times.

Sometimes, however, my anxiety wins the day. Such is life and faith. We intellectually know how to sit deeply, but the upheaval of the moment cannot be overcome. The best I can do is ride awkwardly and frustrate my instructor because my inner emotions are too much for my backside to handle. I flounder my way through a lesson and hopefully stay on the horse. I have discovered that an antidote to my disconnect for sitting deeply in a canter is posting a trot. The movement, I've discovered, gives my anxiety something to do. Like jockeys hovering about the saddle of a racehorse or our human need to busy ourselves with a long list of things to do to distract ourselves from whatever emotion we've decided we'd rather not feel, we engage in movement, sometimes too much.

Jonah reminds me that sitting deeply isn't always about connecting with the most holy parts of myself; it connects me with the real parts of myself. It slows me down to feel what uncomfortable and distasteful feelings I am speeding away from in my life.

Sitting deeply collects me in authenticity. I cannot sit deeply with God and avoid things. I sit deeply with God, pushing down into the dirt of life to discover what has been planted there. I sit deeply with God to get my hands in the muck of life, my human underside, my nature that I've hidden from others and even more dangerously, hidden from myself.

Sitting deeply is a form of prayer, maybe one of humanity's most honest prayers.

Still

Busy yourself with keeping your mind
in the presence of the Lord.
—BROTHER LAWRENCE,
THE PRACTICE OF THE PRESENCE OF GOD[8]

Vacations are restful escapes from day-to-day life: Adventures into new places. Reconnecting with familiar places. Or simply being in a place for a while to live hedonistically for a few days.

Or, at least, they are supposed to be.

I'd hoped my vacation would be a mixture of sleeping late, reading books with no significant philosophical or religious implication, eating chocolate, and exploring. I'd rented a cozy cabin outside Asheville, North Carolina, for some days away. I'd done many of the things I'd planned to do. My time had fits and starts of enjoyment, but mostly I felt jumbled. And when I feel jumbled, I also feel irritated. Shaken and stirred is not my preferred soul condition. I knew something within me was off when I visited three bookstores and left without purchasing a single book.

I'd probably never before left a bookstore without purchasing a book. The stacks of them around my house are proof of that.

Something was off.

The vacation began with an ending. A beloved parishioner had died earlier in the year and, according to her wishes, was interred at a family plot in North Carolina. The family asked if I would do the burial. Of course I would, because there are simply some members who are so profoundly amazing, such a wonderful embodiment of love and grace, that I should get in my car and drive across mountains to pray the prayers of burial, to lower her, with her husband's help, into the ground. I dearly wanted to join her friends and family as we all shoveled dirt upon her grave, until we could replace the grass, pouring the remaining holy water upon the whole business, and see the sunlight shine on a new holy space in an old graveyard.

Then I went on vacation to rest and relax.

But I was shaken and stirred instead of rested and relaxed. Loss and death do that, I reasoned to myself. Officiating the burial of a member I still missed each Sunday as I looked out to her familiar place in the pew and saw emptiness was emotionally draining. I lied to myself about there really being no good books to buy and headed out to the Blue Ridge Parkway to hike instead.

I enjoy hiking in the same way I enjoy lobster, more because every other human being seems to enjoy it, so I should, too. I don't dislike hiking, as I don't dislike lobster. But given a preference, I would choose other things.

But when in Asheville, surrounded by hikers, hiking equipment, and mountains made for hiking in which are etched several thousand hiking trails, I decided to hike. I found a trail marked as a moderately challenging hike that led to some waterfalls. The first mile was more of a race than a hike for me. Outrunning discomfort always seems the better option than walking in its company at the beginning of a potentially uncomfortable journey.

Then I got winded and tired. Outrunning discomfort uphill will do that. So, I slowed to a walking pace. I began to ask myself, "What are the mountains saying to you?" Not so much because I think in questions like that, but because the question seemed like the kind of question women who hiked in the mountains who were cautiously spiritual would ask while they hiked to some ancient waterfalls.

Maybe mountains speak. But I hear the language of horses much more clearly. I wasn't on a horse at the moment, even though the experience reminded me of when I once took Nina on a trail ride. She decided the first two streams she encountered were deadly flows of acid, but by the third one we were good at trotting straight through the water with no dramatic leaps and flairs. She also managed to step into the ribs of a deer carcass along the trail, so I spent some time picking tiny deer bones from her hooves.

Trail riding is not Nina's forte, but it is an adventure with her. *One of the ponies from the barn,* I thought, *would really be excellent on this trail. Then I could ride while the pony walked the trail and listen to the world outside me.* The world outside ourselves has much to say. Most of us are too busy talking, too busy listening for the words we want to hear, that we don't hear what God is saying to us. We fill the space with our own wish lists and complaints so that we miss the silence of God and what wisdom is contained therein.

In the mountains near Asheville by myself, I listened. I didn't think I heard anything profound. I did note some majestic falls, which I stood far above on a scenic overlook all alone, and which were named for a man whose hunting party was massacred on this very spot a century or so ago. The historic marker at the first trail stop noted he and his party were on a hunt that spanned months, and that long hunts were inherently dangerous. This was the historical marker's way of saying they died, but no one was surprised the hunt ended this way.

Linden Falls are stunning, as waterfalls naturally are. Rocks, water, and power focused into one place by gravity tend to have that effect. Then I noticed a small bird sitting on a branch above the gorge. Not an eagle or even a buzzard. Just a random small bird. I sat on an outpost of rocks and watched the bird sit. I wondered about the millions of animals over the eons who'd come to these falls to drink, to hunt, to wander.

The unstunning bird and I sat and watched. More people joined us on the scenic outlook, taking pictures and chattering about plans for lunch. I listened for what the mountains said to me, but heard only the noise of the waterfalls.

I checked the time and realized I could drive over to the Western North Carolina Agricultural Center and see the practice rides. Without much intention, I'd managed to plan some vacation time to coincide with a Saddlebred show in which my barn would show several horses. They would be doing some practice rides in the late afternoon, and I wanted to watch.

As I pulled into the gate of the Center, my phone rang. I didn't recognize the number, so I let it go to voicemail. Once I parked, I listened.

The daughter of another dear parishioner left the message: Mom died early this morning. I listened again. Maybe I'd heard it incorrectly or maybe I wanted magic and God to change this new truth. She wasn't supposed to die yet. Yes, she had a terminal diagnosis and the time was close. But not yet, we'd hoped. I'd met with her only a few days earlier. We'd done the initial plans for her funeral. I'd hugged her before I left and said, "I'll see you when I get back," and she'd replied, "Yes, you will."

But she died. I sat in my car listening to the voicemail from her daughter again, just to make sure I'd heard the words correctly.

I sat in the parking lot of horse stalls at the Western North Carolina Agriculture Center and knew why my soul felt shaken and stirred.

Grief had come to stay for a while. But at that moment I decided I had neither the time nor patience to entertain grief and instead headed to the barn. I found the area where our horses were stalled and chatted with a few of the grooms. A farrier checked the shoes on one of the ponies. I helped clean a saddle and polished my boots. When the last of the show riders arrived, we took Comet, the practice horse, to the ring.

I stood in the middle of the show ring as riders from my barn rode Comet. Before big shows, riders practice to get a sense of the ring, a sense of its size and scope, and how they will ride their horses in their respective classes. They let the show nerves, the excitement of it all, catch up to them on the back of a practice horse so they can better ride their individual show horses.

After all the show riders had taken a turn, Steph told me to get on Comet. I'd ridden him before, but that overanxious part of me as a person and as a rider thought of all the reasons I could say no. This vacation had been less than relaxing, I'd just lost a parishioner and friend, and I was nervous riding in front of big-time show riders.

I listened for what the mountains would say. They didn't say much, still, but the part of my soul that is drawn to the smell and being of horses told me to shut up and ride. So I did. Horses shake and stir me out of my intellect and rational self and into my gut better than any force on earth. I rode this gaited horse— meaning he walks, trots, and canters, and he has two additional gaits, a slow gait and rack. These are four-beat gaits, meaning one of Comet's hooves is on the ground at both of those gaits, but at a higher speed than a walk.

Comet and I rode. Not the best ride I've ever had on him, but the ride I needed to have. He moved me with his energy into the treacherous terrain of grief. Horses are exceptional communicators if we are willing to hear and pay attention to what they are saying to us.

I can say the same about God. I have to be willing to hear what God is saying, and I have to learn how to pay attention. I wasn't willing to do either of those things, then, because I had a deep instinct that God was asking me to grieve.

After the ride and dinner with my barn family, I climbed back into my car. My stomach filled from dinner, and soul rattled and broken from grief, I crested part of the highway to see the sun beginning to set over the mountains. The scene was worthy of the cover of a coffee-table book, stunning and astonishing. I could hear the voice of the woman who'd died saying, "Oh, this is why I love nature."

I heard her voice. And I cried. And not the delicate, hand-me-a-handkerchief-and-I-can-dab-my-eyes cry, but the full-on ugly cry where my face and soul are equally distorted from the pain of what has been lost, and snot falls out of my nose.

I cried because I was heartbroken that I will have to preach yet another sermon for yet another woman I love dearly. I was shaken that I won't see her in the front pews on Sunday ever again or hear her talk about the blue flowers that were rare in the environment due to global warming, but glorious patches were growing in a nature refuge she'd been helping create. I was stirred by the presence of the mountains and the hiking, two things she dearly loved.

I had wanted to avoid the treacherous terrain of grief, and somehow all that day it walked with me into a place where I could finally lament, weep, and grieve. Perhaps the timing was simply right.

Maybe.

I think Comet, in his racking gait that shifted me back and forth, shaking me from my steadfastness in the mantra, "I'm fine," had something to do with shaking my grief free from the corner in which I'd shoved it. Slow gaits and racks in Saddlebreds are great fun to ride, but to ride them well, all parts of a rider's body are engaged in a particular way. I call it the Beyoncé riding style, because hips are moving from side to side and shoulders stay steady and back. It summons a mixture of flexibility and free movement with steady and strong stability.

As I wiped my nose and inhaled the perfect smell of horses that lingered on my coat sleeve, I walked into my cabin and climbed into bed, where I cried some more. I began to realize that I had stored up quite a bit of grief that had been shaken loose.

The next day on my way home, I drove the curving scenic route until I found another hike to a place called Devil's Courthouse, described on the map as a "rambling trail leading to lovely views." So, I hiked upward. And upward. And upward.

I finally rechecked the map to see if this hike ever ended when I realized I was on a "strenuous hike to stunning views." The rambling trail was the hike the next stop down the Parkway. The pages of my guidebook had been stuck together.

Great.

But I was already halfway in, or up, as the trail may be. One foot in front of the other, and I kept walking. Hiking is really walking, just with better views at the end.

Riding a horse is really sitting, just with a moving creature under your backside with a mind and soul of her own. Both seem enticingly easy until you're riding an active, energetic horse or walking up a steep mountain. Then we realize the seductiveness of simplicity.

Feeling grief seems simple. Shed some tears, feel sad, miss them. But our adult grief is rooted in all the losses we've ever felt that even the simple act of admitting we are sad can seem like asking a docile pony for a slow, ambling walk and instead finding ourselves clinging to hang on to the back of a fire-breathing racehorse. We want grief to be contained and predictable. It is instead a sister of the Holy Spirit, behaving more like a three-year-old who's hungry, amped up on sugar, and in need of a nap. And we are the only adult in the room.

Feeling grief, like feeling any holy emotion, is simple. Acknowledging it, sitting with it, allowing it to speak to us— that's the hard work. Grief began to walk with me, and a few final steps and rock formations opened to a cliff-side balcony. Signs advise people to stay on the lookout because, first, we are up really high and plunging to our deaths is not helpful, and second, this is a breeding area for raptors, so don't mess up their nests with your idiocy.

I sat on an outcropping of rocks, maybe the jury box of the Devil's Courthouse. And I listened. I listened to my own soul, to the wind blowing around me, to the silence of the view of four states. The words of Psalm 121 breathed aloud.

I lift up my eyes to the hills; from where is my help to come?

My help comes from the Lord, the maker of heaven and earth.

My help comes from the Lord, the maker of horses and humans, who both bring love into my soul in ways that astonish me and, when that love changes, as it does in death, lacerates me. I sat on the stones of the mountains and let grief sit with me.

I reflected on the past months and days. I suspect people assume that I'm adept at meeting my own grief. I'm not. I intellectualize it and try to normalize it. I want it to fit into a neat box within my life, and I really don't like the way it blows into my life and clears my soul.

I dug into my backpack for some water, an Almond Joy candy bar, and a book of Rumi's poetry. Like horses, a poet from a non-Christian tradition often shifts me from where I am to a new perspective.

I found the poem that speaks of a "crowd of sorrows" violently sweeping through our space. For me, the words of this poem fill in the space between the words of the verse of Psalm 30: Weeping may spend the night, but joy comes in the morning. The psalmist wasn't being literal about time. Yes, weeping does spend the night, and joy does come at dawn, but thinking our grief, anger, or other array of emotions we'd rather stuff under a bed than admit we experience have a twenty-four-hour time clock in our lives is a bit delusional. In between weeping and joy, the violence of upheaval stirs in us, clearing us empty of what feels familiar and wanted.

Delusional though the idea may be, I still harbored hope that I could grieve the loss of two beloved women in a time certain with a clear beginning and a quick and definite ending and move forward, grief-free. I couldn't any more than I could have ridden Comet on my first few riding lessons.

I ate my candy bar and sat with my shaken self. I watched two raptors soar on the thermals from the valley.

Two stunning raptors, soaring. I thought about the two women, soaring in their eternal life with God. I remembered their love, the life they brought to me, and how they had filled my soul with delight.

And for the first time in months, I simply sat deeply in my own grief.

Trust

Over the years, through the experience of several retreats, I've engaged in the spiritual discipline of a trust walk. It's a spiritual discipline for me not to roll my eyes so far back into my head that I see the gray matter of my brain when I hear, "And now we're going to engage our faith in a trust walk!"

If you've never had the experience, allow me to enlighten you. One party is blindfolded, and another party or parties leads the blindfolded person around an area to demonstrate blind faith and trust. The blindfolded party trusts the person guiding isn't a twisted person who thinks a crawl through culverts and across a busy roadway is the point of the exercise.

I have issues with manipulated experiences, but I also realize that our ability to see relates to how much we have need of trust. When I first began riding, I looked downward. I needed to see the horse underneath me. Feeling the horse wasn't enough for me, and this was an almost unconscious action. The conscious action was looking up, looking through the horse's ears, and trusting that this animal on which I'm sitting really is there so I can look up at the world around me.

After a time of learning to see the correct diagonal when I'm posting a trot, the time comes to learn the feel of a correct diagonal. When I first began this exercise of trusting the feel of the horse's hind-end movement with my seat, I experienced the difficulty of trust. Looking down to see if the horse's shoulder and leg next to the wall were going forward as I was posting upward was so much easier. Sitting deeply in the saddle, learning the feel of a certain horse, and rising on the correct diagonal is difficult. Doable, but difficult.

Seeing may be believing, but feeling is what binds trust.

Horses see very similarly to humans, and yet have some striking differences. Because they evolved from animals that grazed on open plains and were often always in sunlight that faded very gradually to darkness, their eyes adapt significantly more slowly from bright light to darkness and vice versa than humans. Leading a horse from a bright paddock into a dark trailer to load or a dim indoor arena without the horse having a slight fit requires trust on the horse's behalf toward the person leading her, since for a while, she can't clearly see her surroundings. Combine this with a horse's natural inclination to be hyper-wary, as they are prey animals (meaning they are not on the top of the food chain), I think horses letting humans lead them into anything without screaming and kicking is slightly south of miraculous.

Our categorical perception differs, as well. Categorical perception is our ability to see things and organize them into groups that make sense to us, often by similar features. If I see a stack of prayer books and hymnals, the prayer books being red and the hymnals being blue, my brain will categorize them by color, really without my awareness. If I see another stack of red books nearby, my brain will have already identified them as prayer books, almost imperceptibly to me.

They may not be prayer books, but I'll have to take a second look to discover that.

Horses, on the other hand, didn't evolve this skill. Janet Jones writes of this, "Horses aren't capable of much categorical perception. And that's why horses notice minor discrepancies in the position of the barn hose. A different view, or the disparate position, of a familiar object is almost the equivalent of a new object."[9]

The environment of life is constantly changing, and horses see that change in a way we humans don't. If the footing in the indoor arena has recently been dragged, creating clean lines in the dirt, a horse will notice. If someone has left a towel on the fence, a horse will notice. If a saddle pad has been hanging on the fence for the first twenty minutes of a ride, but the wind has flipped a part of the pad over, the horse will notice.

While this quality of seeing seems exhausting, when your life in the wild has been as a prey animal, it's a skill that ensured your survival. It's also a skill that leads to horses spooking, spinning, and jumping at threatening things like a flipped-over saddle pad, a sock that a young rider dropped as she left the arena, and a pile of shavings that wasn't there yesterday.

Horses, in their innate brilliance, have learned to trust their rider's vision through their feel. For example, Nina is not a fan of the propane tank that appeared some years ago near the indoor arena. Most of the horses weren't. Our first few trips down to that end of the arena, where the doors were open for the spring breeze, were tedious edging on frustrating. She'd spook. I'd grab mane. I'd push her forward in a walk, trot, or canter—whatever I could do to get her moving in the direction I wanted.

She refused.

Finally, my instructor guided her behind another horse who had decided the propane tank would not, indeed, eat him. Nina, courageous as ever as the second one in line, walked cautiously behind the lead horse, past the evil propane tank, and forward on to our lesson together. She didn't spook again.

Nina saw something different that unsettled her. But her trust in that scary thing was affirmed by my feel. I felt unsettled with her. She didn't want to walk forward because she didn't trust me. My own intimate anxiety seeped from my soul into my skin, through my skin into hers. I was nervous, so she had reason to be nervous.

Never mind that she had seen the tank several times before my instructor finally walked her past it. She didn't trust the feel of it. She didn't trust the feel of me, her rider.

Trust is about feel.

I don't have a high level of trust in institutions, including the church. I did for a long time. I trusted institutions and those who led these institutions. As a member of the church, I trusted those in authority—Sunday School teachers, choir directors, and clergy. The challenge was what I trusted them to do. I trusted them to make decisions good for the gospel and hopefully, when there was intersectionality, for me. What I've discovered as I've lived in this community of faith known as the church is that even those of us who are part of this beautiful mess that is the Christian community often make decisions that have nothing to do with the gospel because we forget to trust the feel of God guiding us, especially when God is guiding us through valleys of the shadow of death and change.

I've watched church leaders who behind closed doors celebrated the full inclusion of LGBTQ people as ordained members of the body of Christ trust, not the feel of shaky courage of love, but the feel of fear that the largest contributors would leave the church. I've edited sermons because I didn't trust the feel of the Holy Spirit leading me to preach the gospel and instead was worrying about how others would react. I've seen the church stand silent in the public forum filled with words clearly antithetical to Jesus's teachings to care for the poor and outcast, trusting instead the euphoria of power.

Trust in God is about feel. Not a deeply comfortable, settling-into-a-recliner feel, but the feel that we are moving forward, led by God, even in our fear and uncertainty. Trust is about feeling God guide us on a new route if we are going into territory that's too dangerous for us, and feeling God push us forward when we decide the territory is too unknown, even dangerous, and God says, "No, trust me, this way is the way of love."

We all can be Nina bopping around the arena of faith and the love of Jesus, doing our best to love God, our neighbor, and ourselves. Then suddenly we see the propane tank of something different, unusual, or unsettling. Maybe we've seen it before, but now it looks slightly different.

We can spook and run away from this new thing in our sight. We can spook and need someone with a bit more sense of God's feel and perhaps more courage to lead us, but we have to be willing to follow. We can spook and remember in the midst of our shakiness that we humans see differently from God who guides us.

We could learn from how horses see the world. When do we need to see things newly, offering ourselves to look at aspects and experiences of our faith we've seen for many circles around our lives, allowing God to shift and change what we see? When are we scared and unsettled by what we see? And in those times, do we feel God guide us in and through these times? Do we remember to trust the feel of God?

Dislodged

The only constant thing in life is change, and things can change rapidly when you're dealing with horses.
—PAT PARELLI,
"THE HORSE IS NEVER WRONG"[10]

*H*orses buck. Some, like Nina, buck rather gently—if a horse dropping her head to throw her hind end up to dislodge a rider could ever be considered gentle. Bucking is a way these very communicative creatures speak to us.

Horses buck naturally. They buck when excited and when playing, as if the joy and exuberance of life is too much to be contained in the body and must be exhaled into the universe through rear legs kicking forth into the world. They buck when scared, throwing strong hind hooves to clear the space behind them of potential predators. They buck when flies bite, when disagreeing with their rider, or when they are otherwise annoyed.

Some horses are bred to buck. Rodeo bucking broncos, for example, are valued for their ability and inclination to buck more readily than other horses. Others regularly buck because they have learned that this behavior gets them what they want.

Or so they think it does.

I do not ride bucking broncos. I ride Saddlebreds. They are not bred for their buck.

But they are opinionated creatures who express their annoyance, at times with a nice moment of saying, "You need to quit riding me!"

And buck.

Bucking dislodges the rider. Always. Your body sitting deep in the saddle is suddenly moving up, and not by your choice. Bucks may send me forward, reins falling free and hands reaching for the horse's mane as something to grab for balance. Feet in stirrups come loose, and perhaps the only thing between me and the ground is pure luck and physics.

Being dislodged is at best annoying and uncomfortable and sometimes dangerous. Our center of balance is upset. We lose contact with our foundations. We may tumble ass over teakettle onto the ground with a painful and unsophisticated thud.

Some horses telegraph a buck, or they may have certain quirks that you may avoid triggering while riding, making them less likely to buck. However, it is an eternal truth that all horses can and will buck. My recovering perfectionist self initially experienced bucking and the subsequent dislodging as a reflection on my riding, which to some extent it is, but not always. I incorrectly believed if I rode the horse just right, if I had the exact mindset, if I held my hands at the perfect level and turned my toes in and dropped my heels, a horse would never buck.

How a person rides a horse can exacerbate a buck, or even cause a buck, but what I need to remember is that horses buck. All of them. The bucking part will happen. What I can control is what I do when I'm dislodged.

Ride long enough, and you will be dislodged from the saddle, sometimes just enough to be annoying, and other times enough to explain your current situation to a medical professional. The first time a horse bucked me, I was terrified. With some good cause. I'm not sure I'll ever be completely okay when the back end of a horse shoots up and out with me in the saddle. But after a few times of it happening, I'm no longer terrified. I realize that being bucked, being dislodged, is one of the many parts of riding.

Horses, God, life, other people's actions, even our own actions, will dislodge us from our center, from the thing that helps us stay where we are. What do I do when my plans and expectations are upended by life, by faith, and by God? What do I do when I'm at a calm walk and encounter someone whose life patterns buck me off my calm? What do I do when I'm dislodged from my comfort zone? How will I respond when I hear the words of Jesus challenge me, dislodge me, and bother me?

My challenge was and is remembering that I am not always living life incorrectly when I'm dislodged. I'm not always doing this life-of-faith thing poorly when I'm dislodged. I may be making poor life choices that dislodge me, and I also may be making good choices that dislodge me.

Life is about being dislodged and how we respond. Life with God is most certainly about being dislodged and how we respond.

If you've never read the Bible, let me sum up about three-quarters of the written accounts: People are living life, sometimes well and sometimes poorly. They encounter God. God dislodges them, usually with some statement or offer to follow God. Life gets unsettled and uncomfortable. People complain—loudly. Whining and wailing and blaming ensues. God listens. People figure out God is in this. People begin living life in this newly dislodged way.

If you've never read any of the accounts of the saints of the Christian faith, let me sum up about 90 percent of their lives: People are living life, sometimes well and sometimes poorly. They encounter God. God dislodges them. Life gets unsettled and uncomfortable. People complain—loudly. Whining and wailing and blaming ensues, although to be fair, some saints respond to being dislodged by deep prayer, by refusing to eat anything but the Holy Eucharist, or by fleeing to the desert for years. They are saints. God listens. People figure out God is in this. People begin living life in this newly dislodged way.

You might see some similarities.

A falsehood of faith is that God wants us to be comfortable, always. We ride along a calm horse on an even path, sitting comfortably in the saddle, while we listen to an old trail song in perfect weather.

A truth of faith is that God is an uncomfortable presence. Being in relationship with God and others dislodges us from our comfortable places, expanding our balance, teaching us newness. Loving our enemy should dislodge us and should bother us. Obedience to love of other people, above our own wants and agendas, should unsettle us. The commandment to forgive seventy times seven should displace us. These are bucks to the system of human behavior and the society our political system encourages.

Our most juvenile faith yearns for God to make everything okay, to smooth the rough waters, to make others whose actions are troubling us conform to how we want them to be, and to be a kindly old gentleman who grants our wishes and whims. This same sense invites us to point and blame, to embrace fully the role of victim, the one who has been completely and utterly wronged. They are related. When we are blaming the other, we almost always cede our power to learn from the event that has dislodged us, waiting instead for God or someone to make everything all okay or to become enamored with perpetually blaming others.

A more experienced, mature faith, one that has seasoned in heartbreak, deep wounds, and the uncomfortable experience of holy healing, recognizes God as a presence with us on the rough waters, incarnate in those whose actions are troubling us and granting us God's will be done, even when we haven't fully considered the upheaval of what following God's will means in our lives. We will certainly encounter moments and people who dislodge us in our life, whose bucking upsets or deeply injures us. Such is life. Horses buck. People buck.

God, quite honestly, likes to buck us to dislodge us from stagnation, from patterns that are not loving or kind to ourselves or others, from staying a perpetual victim of life's changes and chances, and from our own self-made cocoons. God's bucks are sometimes gentle, reminders to pay attention to the moment. Often, the gentle bucks lead to moments that truly dislodge us, to invite us to a new awareness, a new learning.

Every rider has that horse, the one who knows all your bad habits. Inevitably, my instructor asks me to ride this horse during a week when I've dealt with that particular person, that situation, or that moment in life when I'm almost at the end of my rope. Fussy, bucking horses have a profound way of providing insights to our own fussiness, our own needs to buck against life. And they speak the perfect language that forces us to sit in the muck of our souls and wrap ourselves in humility.

When I'm riding a horse I know has a propensity for peppering her rides with bucks to express her opinion about how I'm riding or whether or not she cares to canter at a particular speed, I stay prepared.

Mostly.

I pay attention for her signals, the movement of her tail or the drop of her head. Horses will communicate to you what they are considering, if you are listening. When I hear her tail swish, I can (on a good day) slightly touch her rein or pull my legs away from her side or adjust in some way to change her mind and my approach. I can listen to my instructor talk me through a buck.

Attuning my awareness to the signs that a horse is preparing to buck reinforces the importance of attuning myself to the signs that I'm being dislodged by the actions of another, that their words and deeds are unsettling to me, sometimes in a helpful, holy way. When I'm faced with a new understanding, another perspective that challenges and even changes mine, those are helpful moments of being dislodged from the firmly set and concretely mixed parts of my soul that need to be broken open.

We are also dislodged by hurtful choices of others. This day, I brushed a new horse who'd recently come to live at the barn, and I mulled the moments that had happened in the past weeks. I saddled Scout for a first ride. He is an older, calmer horse. Scout has seen the world and has his thoughts about it, mostly how he can do his job and not exert too much energy. As we rode around the arena at different gaits, me paying attention to tiny placement issues, my own bucking soul calmed. We'd ridden well for about forty minutes. He rode steady and solid.

So when he dropped his head and bucked with authority, I was caught off guard.

Before my brain realized what had happened, I had Scout in a nice trot halfway around the ring. He could buck, and I could still ride. I even discovered I could resettle myself in the saddle while he was moving forward.

Enough bucks in life, and maybe I'd realized being dislodged is simply part of this rodeo life of spirituality, relationships, and riding. My own bucking made Scout's moment less scary for me, more a moment between rider and horse that asked me to shift and change, even if I wasn't fully clear on what Scout was telling me.

Were my hands too stiff? Had he not appreciated the tap of the crop urging him to step up his trot? Was he simply seeing what I would do? Scout wasn't sharing any answers with me, but I knew how I could respond. I could sit deeply, go forward, and guide.

Could I do the same with me?

I found my own soul bucking against people who were pulling too much on my soul, kicking me in my side as they asked me to perform for them as they demanded. An older couple I knew from my first days in Lexington were grabbing on the reins of myself and soul and pulling hard. We'd met at a dinner party of a mutual friend and spent time in conversation because their daughter, about my age, had moved to the town from which I just moved. They asked questions about things their daughter could do in my former town, and I enjoyed hearing the exciting adventures that waited exploration of my new town. They offered to take me on a tour of hidden gems of the Bluegrass area around Lexington, especially one of the historic distilleries where the wife worked as a volunteer. They would, over the course of the months, text, call, and email me weekly, invite me over for dinner, and bring me gifts—"little happies," the wife called them.

Over this same course of months, what began as a friendship started to feel oppressive. One evening over dinner, they shared with me how much they loved me, how they considered me their adoptive daughter. I felt smothered by these waves of unwanted affection. I did not want to be their adoptive daughter. I have my own parents and my own fair share of issues concerning them. I'd tried, gently in my mind but probably vaguely, to place some boundaries. I begged off the weekly dinners and explained that I didn't need "little happies" or five birthday cards for one birthday.

They would, in turn, nod and continue, and I would sigh and continue. I wondered if this is how all the wayward children of fairy tales who get seduced into a gingerbread cottage, only to find themselves consumed, feel before they step through the threshold decorated with peppermint sticks.

Then one day, when they happened to walk into the same restaurant a date and I were dining at and invited themselves to sit down and join us, I found my limit. The next day I shared my deep frustration, except it likely wasn't as soft and gentle as I'd hoped.

I told them I would not be joining them for dinner again, I would not accept any more gifts, and they were not welcome to interfere in my life. Period.

They were upset with my declarations and asked what they'd done wrong. I was only too happy and angry to share all that they'd done wrong, and I ended my litany with, "You have no respect for my boundaries." I'm quite certain I was pointing my finger at them, too.

The trained counselor in me shivers a bit at that sentence. "You" is almost never a helpful declaration during an argument. They experienced, correctly, that these boundaries were a rejection of the way they wanted to be in relationship. I'd strangled at the bit for too long, ignored the discomfort I'd felt, and allowed myself to be, in my feelings, used as a surrogate daughter in ways that felt abusive to me.

So, I bucked.

Bucking is a way our souls communicate with ourselves and others. When something is too much, we buck. We dislodge another from their place in our lives, and our own bucks dislodge us. This moment dislodged me from what felt like being their adopted possession into my own skin again. It wasn't the best option, perhaps, and I still feel a bit sheepish about how angry I was and how, subsequently, I've never spoken to them again. My buck clearly dislodged them and likely hurt them as well.

It dislodged me, too. I'd ignored the signs in my own soul of discomfort and annoyance, of something being wrong in this relationship. We humans, I realize, buck naturally. Our primal souls don't always have the patience or ability to share in soft, comfortable ways the exuberance of life or the anger of life. Or our souls have become too enamored with the way things are to step outside our comfort zone, so God bucks us.

However we are dislodged, after we shake off the trauma or discomfort of the moment, we have a response. For me, I asked myself why I had ignored the signs for too long, why I had not spoken my truth. Would it have dislodged them anyway? Probably.

Would we still be in relationship? I'm not sure. My sense is that I had accepted a role they wanted me to fill that would not have ever been comfortable for me.

I think that my bucking self is an intensely authentic part of me, a holy part of me that wants me to pay attention. That truth is itself a dislodging moment. I want to be nice, sweet, and gentle.

A woman who bucks may be some of those sometimes, but she certainly isn't some of those all the time. She is a bit wild and tempestuous. She is a bit unpredictable, and touch her mane a certain way or push her forward in the wrong manner and you will hear about it.

Since humans are made in the image of God, perhaps this all should be no surprise. God, after all, unvarnished and stripped of the paint of our eons of projections, is wild and unsettling. Our attempts to bridle the Spirit have been futile. Our ideas to explain God completely have always been kicked away.

Horses buck. Humans buck. God bucks.

To be in relationship with any and all of these means we must always be ready to be dislodged and always be willing to ask ourselves, in the aftermath of being dislodged, *Now what?*

Humility

*For all who exalt themselves will be humbled, and those
who humble themselves will be exalted.*

—LUKE 14:11

I was riding during the second week of Advent,
a season of waning light, growing darkness, and waiting. The
church joins Mary (or Miriam, as her Hebrew family and friends
would have called her) in holding the Christ child within,
waiting for the birth.

We in the church can romanticize waiting. I've heard sermons
and read essays that lift up waiting in a way that disconnects
from the reality of our lives. Sit for hours waiting to renew your
driver's license or car tag. Wait on someone who is late, late, late
for an appointment and you have a busy day scheduled. Wait
on the cable people to come sometime during that three-hour
window they give for service.

Now tell me how wonderful waiting is.

That is waiting. At its best, we feel annoyed and frustrated by waiting. Maybe some can find a Zen place. Others bring a book and occupy their time. But honestly, waiting feels like a waste of time.

Yet we drape it with affectionate projections. We do the same with humility, another key aspect of faith that gets center stage during Advent. Miriam was humble, we preach and sing. We sing in the hymn *The Angel Gabriel* that gentle Mary bowed her head, an oft-seen image of humility.

But humility is not an aspect of a pushover faith. Mary may have bowed her head, but she also interrogated the angel Gabriel. She stood and faced the Crucifixion when the disciples hid under beds and in dark corners.

We distort humility as something wrapped in sweetness and gentleness, forgetting the deeply intuitive courage humility takes for humans to succumb to this holy exhortation.

As a quality of faith, humility, like waiting, is not a particularly exciting or validating experience. Humility reminds us that we have much to learn.

I was learning that today. Again.

The appropriately named horse Maria was teaching me, again, a lesson in humility.

I've ridden her for years. She and I usually ride with each other, building on each other's strengths as horse and rider. She's not a fan of heavy hands pulling on her mouth. I'm not sure any horse truly likes having her mouth yanked and jerked, but some are less tolerant of the bad riding habit than others. She is a fan of riders who sit back and heavy, who guide her and step her up to her best.

She's taught me well over the years, how to ride with steady, quiet hands and how to communicate clearly what I would like her to do.

During those lessons, she's run off with me a few times. One particularly unsettling lesson, when I was at a point in my life when I believed I didn't know how to canter a horse anymore, had me in tears in my car at the end of the lesson. But that was then, and in the present we'd developed quite a lovely riding relationship with each other.

Until this evening.

Maria and I were trotting together well. And then I asked her to canter. I started the canter off wrong. Too heavy in my hands, asking for the canter too close to a wall, and I was leaning forward. Maria took about four strides nicely, then went off to the races. She galloped and even bucked a few times. I kept leaning forward, losing my seat every time she communicated her displeasure with me in a subtle yet clear buck. Which, of course, made me more anxious and less of a helpful rider to her.

Rides like this make me wonder how my instructor doesn't use more profanity during a lesson; that day she watched me ride a canter as if I'd never seen a horse before.

After several ugly, failed attempts at the canter, with my pride cast in a smoldering pile in the corner of the arena, Maria and I trotted around the ring, in cooperation with each other.

At least we finished well.

After the lesson, Steph called me to the center and asked me, "Why do you get so anxious? Even now, you're fussing with her reins and annoying her. Stop it."

Why do I get so anxious?

Probably because I'm a recovering perfectionist. Anxiety and perfectionism are neighbors on the same street of unhelpful qualities that our culture rewards. When we realize we have much to learn, even relearn, anxiety and perfectionism cloak this in shame, as if we should be all-knowing. So too often we fake what we don't know, wrapping ourselves in hubris and egoism.

Horses and God counter both of those with humility and waiting.

Somewhere in the lexicon of faith, anxiety and perfectionism stand in contrast to waiting and humility.

Anxiety and perfectionism fill me with worry and unreasonable standards. I move without intention in order to have something to do, to have expectations that are unrealistic and unhelpful, and to allow the words of my brain to take center stage with no regard to settling deeply in my body. In faith and riding, my anxiety and perfectionism have a narrow list of what is acceptable and expected, and if those outcomes don't happen, in my view I'm a failure and I have disappointed God. This shows up most beautifully when I show horses. If I don't win, the recording in my soul hits the play button: *You don't know how to ride. You're a disappointment to the barn. You'll never be an accomplished rider. Why do you even try?*

This same dialogue chattered on during my time in church in high school and, for a while, in college. I could never live up to the standards I'd experienced in the church of my childhood and youth. The superstar Christians in my youth group testified to their Jesus experiences at our annual youth revivals and during summer mission trips, while I felt woefully inadequate with my own experience of Christ. When the altar call happened at church, I was tired of being the only one of my friends who hadn't dedicated their life to Christ, so I went, not because my soul felt strangely warmed, but because I didn't want to be the only nonsaved person in my group of friends. Hell would be rather lonely for me if all my friends were saved and I wasn't. When I asked questions about the Bible we studied so diligently in church—questions like, "Why are there two creation stories?" and "So where does it say dancing is a sin in the Bible?"—I was met with a challenge to my faith by my elders.

Another sentence to add to the recording: *If you had enough faith, you wouldn't question.*

The standard of perfection is a whisper of evil. It taunts us as a possibility. You, yes *you* can be the best! You can have no blemish or error. You can be a winner all the time. If someone says you hurt them, *they* are the ones who are wrong. You can be perfect, just as Christ was perfect!

Except we aren't perfect. Jesus is. We aren't. We make mistakes. We make wrong choices that hurt those we love and ride with our hands too heavy on the reins and so we annoy the horse. We have moments when we amaze with our gifts, and we have moments that make our instructors swear with our inability to keep our shoulders back and open. We think we can earn our way into love if we're just good enough, forgetting that love is not earned.

God is already ahead of us, choosing not the perfect paragons of faith to be matriarchs and patriarchs, but those who were dazzlingly imperfect. They wander for decades, argue with God, wrestle with angels, and question the Divine. Along the way, they have sex with their daughters, get smashingly drunk, pass a wife off as his sister to save his skin, and deny knowing Jesus in his hour of great need.

They stumble upon their faith and the grace of love, not because they strive for perfection, thus allowing anxiety to fill the spaces in their souls, but because they offer themselves to humility.

Humility, being humbled, is a part of riding . . . and a foundational part of faith.

The origins of the word relate to the earth, to the mucky dirt under our feet. Humility is a downward movement for our souls and for our egos. When we are humbled, we remember and acknowledge that we indeed are not all that and a bag of chips. We do not have all the answers. We are not infallible. We still have much to learn.

Mary in her hymn *Magnificat* sings:

He hath shewed strength with his arm: he hath scattered the proud in the imagination of their hearts. He hath put down the mighty from their seat: and hath exalted the humble and meek. (Luke 1:51 KJV)

God exalts the humble and meek. Not so much, I think, by infusing them with outrageous pride or pretensions, but by reminding us that humility is a holy quality. Being humble in my life and faith allows me to be grounded in my identity, beloved of God as I learn, as I discover my ways of doing things might not be the only way. Humility sits me back down on the ground, close to the dirt of creation that God formed and breathed over to create humanity.

Humility can also be understood as humbleness of mind. This particular aspect reminds me of my position in God's creation as part of creation, not the entirety of it. Or, more accurately, not to think more highly of myself than I ought. Humbleness of mind is a writ-large reminder that I will never know everything I need to know, and what I do know is tempered with the knowledge that I will always need to learn more, and God and horses are always willing to be the teachers.

Humility in our relationships with God and each other and with horses nudges us, pokes us, and even yells at us to recognize what we don't know and what we need to open ourselves to learn.

Every single time I get on a horse, I am humbled. Sometimes in small ways, and sometimes in large, writ-bold-across-the-sky ways. Humility, when it's running away with me and bucking in a gait I've ridden for years, does not feel welcome.

Humility feels uncomfortable and bruising to our egos. Reminders that we are fallible, that we are mistaken, that we are not as smart as we think we are or as competent as we hope we are crack the exterior images we have often worked so hard to portray to the world. God, in holy strength, scatters our images of perfection, control, and superiority by running wild.

Perhaps that is why we respond with bucks when God humbles us in our relationships with others. When someone shares with us that our words or actions have hurt them, are we more inclined to learn from what we are hearing in another's truth, or are we inclined to buck and push back, defending ourselves from any hint that we have not been perfect?

Why am I so anxious?

Because I forget that I am a beautiful mess, that I have much to learn about love and riding, and that I am not perfect.

I forget that God finds me in this state and sings a hymn of the grace of humility to me. Today it just happens to be in the form of a bucking horse. But I hear the music, and I sit deeply. Humility sits, kneels, and bows. Humility reaches down to the earth. Humility remembers I have much to learn.

Humility waits as God teaches me.

Envy

$\mathcal{I}$ felt a pang of envy when I listened to Anita gush about riding her new horse, Rosie, in a show. She absolutely glowed as she shared putting on the coat and derby of show fashion, climbing in the saddle, and riding with Rosie around the show ring. The envy wasn't because Anita was riding in the performance level of showing, the next level available to me. The envy wasn't that Anita won her class. She didn't even place.

I felt envy at the sheer joy Anita felt riding her horse. I felt envy at the energy Anita had, not from winning, but from being present in the moment of showing a beautiful horse on a summer evening in Kentucky. A ribbon would be nice, but the win was the joy she felt riding her magnificent horse, Rosie, around a ring, both working together to shine.

Envy appears in the lineup of the seven deadly sins, a list compiled by early Christians, likely related to ethical lists of the Greek world. I don't find these lists particularly helpful, because they consist mainly of emotions, and emotions themselves are not good or evil as much as they simply *are*. What we do with our emotions can be quite evil or good.

Covetousness, envy's first cousin, appears in the list of the Ten Commandments, reminding men not to crave or desire their neighbor's material possessions, including their wives and their livestock. The biblical sense of envy and covetousness seems related, not to a simple desire to wanting something, but to wanting something at the expense of someone else having it. I once heard a preacher suggest that envy is the root of what moves the economy. I see a pair of shoes a friend is wearing. I would like to have them. I go buy the same style shoes. Nothing particularly evil about that.

The Bible, however, focuses on the hurtful side of envy. I see the shoes and engage in gossip and speculation about how my friend got the shoes, or I steal them from her. This form of envy rots relationships. I can imagine a man a few thousand years ago coveting one of his neighbor's wives and a few of his goats and organizing an invading party to steal said wife and goats. The victim of the raid misses his one wife of a dozen or so and his few goats of a hundred, and retaliates. Humans seem inclined to seek retribution instead of understanding and forgiveness. Soon there's a border war, and chaos ensues.

We can see why jealousy, covetousness, desire, and envy can cause problems for peace, love, and harmony in a community.

What might happen, however, if we let our feelings of envy inform us of a deep desire in our soul, something in another we ourselves want to cultivate or attain, not at the expense of another, but for our own growth? Then, envy becomes a messenger from our deep subconscious about what we may value and yearn for. When we see another with that, whatever *that* may be, instead of admitting we yearn for it, I wonder if we, with no interest in being bucked out of wherever we are into newness, twist this yearning into jealousy.

Poet Rainer Maria Rilke wonders, "Perhaps all the dragons in our lives are princesses who are only waiting to see us act, just once, with beauty and courage. Perhaps everything that frightens us is, in its deepest essence, something helpless that wants our love."[11]

Sometimes what we envy may be a desire, a need, a yearning that has helplessly been cast off in our souls and wants to be loved into recognition. If we let the dragon of envy lead us down deeply into ourselves, we may discover not only something we want, but something of ourselves that needs our love.

My envy of Anita wasn't about her showing at performance level, or having a beautiful show horse, or the great community that grew from days at horse shows out of town (well, maybe I have some jealousy about that). When I sat with my envy, especially when I sat with the feeling while I rode in my show classes, I realized I wanted her joy just from showing, the enthusiasm and elation she had simply from riding a horse in front of judges.

The challenge of following envy deep down is a journey that goes through the muck of our issues. We almost always feel the flash of envy and associate it with the person or thing closest to us. We may not like a person who is new in our congregation, because she has interesting ideas about children's ministry. We may feel envy toward other choir members because we don't like the way, our surface pride says, they are showy with their voices. We grab on to the low-hanging fruit that our pride offers us that allows us to be righteous in that nonbiblical way.

Jesus enjoys pushing us deeper into our mud and muck, past our self-righteousness into loving transformation. We get upset because we're not even sure what we've hidden underneath all the muck in our souls that envy has deposited in a steaming pile into our lives. Jesus, never one to be afraid of the seedy underbelly of humanity, including our very own souls, hands us a pitchfork and a muck bucket and offers to help us dig.

And we dig. Maybe we discover we're scared that the new fabulous member who has different ideas about children's ministries will make us seem irrelevant. Maybe the other voices in the choir mean we might not get all the solos. Maybe the envy of watching a friend's show reminded me of a joy I rarely felt when I showed horses.

Envy, like anger, is *sad*'s bodyguard. Feeling sad feels vulnerable. Envy and anger? They are close relatives that give us a sense of power, albeit fragile, unhelpful power that tears down rather than builds up.

I had gone through a couple of years of showing where joy was the last thing I felt. When I showed a horse, I was instead anxious, stressed, and tense. Horses, being the empaths they are, feel all those emotions, which clearly prevent both horse and rider from doing our best. After I left the ring on the day of my envy, frustrated at my performance, I did a postmortem on the ride and realized I felt sadness.

Richard Rohr notes, quite correctly, that we're all addicts, but some of us have socially acceptable addictions.[12] Mine is, as I've mentioned, being a perfectionist. I've heard a litany of why perfectionism becomes a part of someone's personality, particularly women. We live in an achievement-oriented culture that rewards winners, with certificates hanging on our walls, degrees from prestigious universities, and titles. We learn from an early age that people laud us for achieving, and we equate that attention with love. And we find that gathering accomplishments validates us. I might feel like a hot mess on the inside. *But look at all this stuff I've achieved, won, and earned,* we think. *Therefore, I must be a good person.*

God blows this very human idea of worth to bits. Throughout the stories of the patriarchs, the second sons, those who did not inherit titles or lands according the rules of society, were the ones lifted to prominence. Jesus had little energy for the rich and powerful, dining instead with the kind of people who possessed criminal records rather than degrees from snazzy colleges. Our faith confesses and preaches and reiterates that we can do nothing to earn God's love, that we as humans are beloved by God simply because God chooses to love us.

Intellectually knowing that truth and living it are far different realities. For many of us, love is conditional and something that feels earned. This earned love may have aspects of love, but it isn't purely God's love. I heard this well described by a friend in recovery: "If I bake cookies for you because I want to share chocolate-chip cookies with you out of appreciation and care, that's love. If I bake cookies for you so you will love me and owe me, that's codependence."

In her language, codependence is the idea that we can earn love. That idea ran deeply and strongly through ancient cultures and their various gods and goddesses who regularly needed sacrifices and offerings of things to curry their favor. People who amassed wealth, power, and large families were often deemed blessed, and the thread of this particular human understanding of love weaves through the biblical narrative into our modern faith.

People win awards, land a big business deal, buy their new 2,700-square-foot dream home, or invest in just the right stock portfolio and describe themselves as "blessed by God."

As if God hands out Grammys, blue ribbons, and financial windfalls to express holy love. We might be more accurate in saying we are fortunate when these things happen, and admit we are still working through our tendency to couch God's love in codependent terms.

So yes, we easily equate accomplishments with validation and validation with love. Jesus enjoys the continual process of handing us pitchforks, shovels, and muck buckets as we dig into the shit of our souls. While riding horses gives me insight and wisdom that mostly feels affirming, my recovering perfectionist self finds a huge place of growth in horse shows.

"Dig in," says the Lord of Hosts.

Riding is, in and of itself, a strange way to feel accomplished. My instructor often asks me after a lesson, "Do you feel accomplished?" She's figured me out, that I occasionally need to find some gold-star moment while riding in my regular lessons. Sometimes I feel accomplished because I stayed on a horse. Other times I realize I'm feeling more comfortable working the arena instead of simply riding securely on the rails all the time, and that sense of broader vision pats me on the back. I get less anxious when I experience a nonaccomplishment moment, like a horse who isn't responding to my cues and not participating in the program of the day.

Then we have horse shows, overflowing with competition and ribbons. It's a candy store of validation with rosettes and streamers and trophies. Saddle-seat competition is a rather interesting competition. Unlike eventing, where horses run a timed course and have to clear jumps to place, or jumping, where horses jump various obstacles cleanly to win, saddle-seat competition is more subjective. I liken it to a ballet competition I once saw. There are clear markers: Is your horse doing the gaits as called? Are you, in equitation, posting on the correct diagonal? These are some of the standards. But other factors are subjective to the judge. What looks elegant and powerful at the same time, how collected the horse is, and even how the rider looks on the horse are some of the subjective standards.

This can all be frustrating to me as a rider. I often wonder if my competitive "I like to win" streak, and "please give me a ribbon so I can have external validation that I'm a good rider" self, have met their match in saddle-seat competition.

I toss a pile of manure into the bucket as Jesus says, "Yes."

I can get far too focused on the win. The past year had not been a good show season for me. I hadn't won a single show, and my frustration level increased until one day, I realized I was so anxious before and during a show that I had no memory of even showing the horse.

Even worse, I'd not felt joy. Any joy. I wasn't even happy that I'd not fallen off the horse during a competition. Which matters, because I won a class once because I was the only rider to stay on my horse. Little things are always big things at the right moment.

When I looked at the pictures from the last show, I realized that even if I'd won the class (I ended up second), it would have been a loss. The pictures were amazing. Glory was trotting, legs high, head set. She looked beautiful. Stunning. And all I remember was being frustrated and scattered. I didn't help her one bit, because I was too caught up in whatever annoyance I was feeling at the time. I didn't settle in with her and ride her so we both could shine.

I realized she looked beautiful almost in spite of me, not because of me.

Listening to Anita, I knew what I'd missed. Maybe what I'd forgotten. The win isn't measured in a ribbon (although make no mistake, place ribbons are just lovely). The win is measured in feeling joy in the ride.

I took most of the last show season off, stepping away. I wondered if I'd miss it.

I didn't miss showing as much as I thought, but part of me wondered if I'd taken the easy way out. Avoidance is almost never a long-term solution for the things that upend our spirituality.

So, I showed again, after almost a year. I didn't win then, either. In fact, my dear, stunning Maria didn't cooperate at the walk in the way the judge seemed to want. But we did a few things we hadn't done together. When I'd shown her a year earlier, she all but ran away with me at one of the gaits. Not so this time. I was more attentive to my place in the ring. And our canter starts were collected and smooth.

And I felt joy in our ride. I thought, as we left the ring with our ribbons that were not in the top three, *How many women get to ride a stunning, sassy horse around a ring on a Saturday, working with her to shine?*

Not many.

But I do.

I get to climb in the saddle dressed in a show suit and ride. I get to show judges, not that I'm the best rider, but that I love being on a horse, that I can work with the horse so we both look our best on that day.

I hadn't done that in a long while. I've ridden for the win, for perfection, for something other than joy. Riding for the win isn't joyful. Winning is a fleeting moment that ends when you get off the horse. Because win or lose, I'll go back to working on my riding skills with the horse on Monday.

If I'm not enough without the blue ribbon, I'll never be enough with it.

Envy is the bodyguard of this truth—that if we don't feel enough without the thing we desire that another has, having it won't help us feel worthier. Why on earth God decided to let envy be a place to rest the barriers to the commandment to love ourselves will be on my list of questions to ask someday.

But for now, I don't get to ask that question. I do get to ask God to help me dig into my envy and uncover the self-worth God wants me so much to embrace, the self-worth God wants every human to embrace. We forget the commandment is to love our neighbors as ourselves. I actually think most humans love their neighbors as much as they love themselves, which is not very much. To love ourselves means knowing who we are, exploring the wonderful aspects of us and the "quick, hide those because company's coming" aspects of us. Doing so takes courage, faith, and community.

In the late fall, I climbed back on a horse and entered another show ring. This time I rode Nina, and I laughed as I rode. Some hard work in the off season digging into my own deep mud and muck seemed to have rearranged a few things. I couldn't tell you exactly how and what I'd done, but I suspect time in the saddle and time with God eventually changes us without our conscious awareness. I remember almost every step Nina and I made together that day in the show. We lined up to hear our results.

Anita won. And I came in second.

I recognize that I'll likely always struggle with the need for validation when I show, always get the wires crossed between having a good ride and winning, in the same way we humans will probably always struggle with the truth that God loves us because of and despite of ourselves, not because we earn love. But for the first time in a while, I didn't need a ribbon to feel joy in the time I'd spend with a horse. I didn't need a ribbon to feel accomplished.

I just needed to ride.

Love

I came so close to Love
That I began to know
What is won by all those
Who give themselves wholly to Love...
—HADEWIJCH[13]

My first real memory of a relationship with riding horses is of not riding them. I was in first or second grade, and like most Southern girls of that time, I was a Brownie, part of the Girl Scout program. This Brownie meeting was an adventure on a farm. We bottle-fed lambs. We saw chickens and gathered some eggs, all events less thrilling to me who had grandparents and great uncles with farms than my fellow Brownies who lived in the suburbs. We petted goats and felt their sprouting horns. I still remember the pungent, musky smell of the older male goats.

I remember not being able to ride a horse.

The last part of our farm tour was a horse ride. Each girl got to sit in a saddle and ride the horse as her trainers led her down and back in a paddock. Each girl got to ride.

Each girl except me.

My parents didn't sign the permission form. I had to stand alone that day, the one girl who didn't get to ride. Another girl brought me a flower to cheer me up. I said, "Thank you," then the Girl Scout leader told me to smile. I didn't want to, and didn't. Thus ensued the lecture from the leader about being nice and smiling even when I didn't feel like it.

Along with the repugnant smell of male goats, the Brownie farm tour left me with the reinforcement of the repugnant lesson that my feelings don't matter. So what if I felt disappointment and anger? Smile and say, "I'm fine."

I remember being angry that my parents hadn't signed a permission slip, that their lack of action left me on the rail, watching others. I was disappointed that I couldn't ride the bay horse, walking down and back. I wanted to ride her, to sit in that saddle, and be part of her walk. Instead, I rested my seven-year-old forehead against a fence rail and watched each girl take her turn riding a horse down the paddock and back. I wanted fiercely to cry, but the words of the woman pinched the inside of my soul, their force willing my tears away. I told myself aloud, "You don't want to cry. You must smile instead."

And so I did. Each girl who ran down the fence and stood next to me, talking with all the energy young girls do about their exciting ride, I met with a forced smile troweled over my real feelings. I don't remember love on that day, my first cognitive memory of horses. I don't even remember love the first day I stepped into a Kentucky barn, almost four decades later. I do remember wondering how much Advil I'd need to take after each lesson. I still buy it in bulk: one of the horsewoman's requirements.

I signed my own permission slip this time. I even had to sign a waiver. Riding horses is a risky endeavor that can result in death and/or dismemberment, so sign here.

There were no fences or small ponies on which I would ride in a straight line down and back, then get off and let someone else have a turn. There was an indoor arena, and I would ride in a large oval. And not only at a walk, but also at a trot.

I introduced myself to the instructor. She was cheerful and asked if I'd ever ridden before.

"Yes, but Western. Not in this," I responded, noting the saddle on the back of the horse that resembled a leather potato chip. I doubted whether my ample rear would fit, I joked. She laughed. I laughed that laugh people do when they aren't sure if the situation was funny or the prelude to a tragedy.

"So why did you decide to ride?"

Because I was afraid of losing myself, of realizing my entire life was filled, top to bottom and side to side, with all things work, leaving no room for the human being that is Laurie. I was afraid I was unlearning the lessons I'd learned over the past years, after the emotional upheaval, the stripping away of all things I thought worked for me, the church breaking my heart, and my own resurrection, complete with emotional scars that were mostly healed but still ached when the weather changed.

I surmised that answer, however, was a bit more detailed than this instructor I'd just met needed to hear, so I told her I made a New Year's resolution to get more active, and I hated going to the gym.

Which is actually true, just not the whole truth and nothing but the truth.

Then, I rode.

After my first few lessons, I realized I'd found something I had no idea I was searching for in my life. God is like that, I think, showing up in places and people and horses in surprising ways, and we respond, "Oh, there you are!" because we know immediately this was the thing missing. Only after we've engaged and brought something of our soul to the surface we didn't even know we'd lost do we realize what resurrection truly looks like in our lives.

Maybe if I'd ridden down and back that day so many years ago I would have been that child who never wanted to get off a horse. Maybe I would have hated the ride. Who knows?

I know that when I felt the presence of too many things in my life, my soul went on a search to a barn, and I gave myself permission to follow. Horse riding simply felt right, or at least easy in the horse capital of the world, as Lexington bills itself, and when an online coupon for five horseback-riding lessons appeared in my email, I thought, *Why not?* I didn't know anything about saddle-seat riding or Saddlebreds other than that they were horses and I wanted to ride horses.

Faith and love seem to grow best in the dirt of not knowing. I went one day to ride horses, not knowing I would find love and in that love an expression of God.

Paul's hymn to love in chapter 13 of the First Letter to the Corinthians is eloquent. "Love is patient; love is kind; love is not envious or boastful or arrogant or rude. It does not insist on its own way; it is not irritable or resentful; it does not rejoice in wrongdoing, but rejoices in the truth. It bears all things, believes all things, hopes all things, endures all things. Love never ends."

For me right now, love is Nina, four legs with a tiny dot of white on her nose where I kiss her. Love is our routine of me putting my riding gloves on the ledge in her stall and her picking them up with her mouth and dropping them on the floor because she can. Love is the never-ending supply of peppermints Nina is sure I have in my pockets. Love is even digging out the poo she has deposited in her food pail because she's unhappy with the state of affairs at the barn, usually that her feed has been changed or she wants more hay.

Love is the confidence I have on her now even to ride her bareback and the way I enjoy riding her when she's in a truly bitchy mood because her show-horse pedigree is very evident then with her long neck, collected steps, bright ears, and attitude.

Love is the way we nuzzle each other at the end of a day, and the smell of her I hope is the smell of heaven. Love is the moment I've struggled to ride a particular horse and, after far too many rides that leave me feeling unsettled, I finally have *that* ride, the one that pushes me into a new place in my riding ability. Love is the horse that bucked and the one that didn't. Love is the horse who reminded me to sit deep and the one who hates being touched on her side with my legs.

Love is each lesson, even a fleeting moment, when I am wholly and completely embraced in the moment with another one of God's creatures. Love is the neck of a horse, which receives nuzzles of love and tears of heartbreak better than any handkerchief or tissue. Love is my barn family who knows a part of me that is grounded in boots, covered in horse hair and hay, and shovels muck for fun.

Love is showing up, day in and day out, to ride, to learn, to be part of the life and story of the horse and God.

Love demands chance, failure, falling, and endurance. Our love of God and God's love for us is not safe in the traditional sense. It asks us to fall deeply into risky truth. For me, God's love smells of church incense and beeswax candles and horses and hay. God's love is steadfast as it moves within, around, and underneath me, asking me to move with it. This love stretches, collects, and balances me.

Love is knowing that the brightness of the Son can be blinding, so we rarely dare to stare directly into the face of God. But we can see the love of God reflected in things in our life. We find this reflection of the light of holy love in different things. I found God's holy love reflected in horses and the community that surrounds all things related to them. From my instructors who guide me and teach me, to my barn family who laughs with me and nourishes the part of me that needs simply to be human, to Nina, who nuzzles me after long days, love is patient, kind, and enduring.

This love, this wise, deep, ancient love, is the love told to me by horses, in the way that only horses can speak of God.

Words (again)

*One of the most important—and most neglected—
elements in the beginnings of the interior life is the
ability to respond to reality, to see the value and the
beauty in ordinary things, to come alive to the splendor
that is all around us in the creatures of God.*
—THOMAS MERTON[14]

I have had an eternal and inconsistent relationship
with horses most of my life, not unlike my relationship with
God. God and horses have been faithfully present, even when
my attention has been focused elsewhere. From Western riding
lessons and youth-group prayer circles to trail rides on bomb-
proof Quarter horses and revivals that recharged my faith,
horses and God were the deep, solid earth under the foundation
of my life.

Humans are connected to spiritual expression, whether we
acknowledge and nurture that connection or not. We've been

spiritual in one way or another as long as we've been humans. Anthropologists recognize human spiritual expression reaching back some three hundred thousand years, with our burying the dead. Evidence of rituals with those burials followed; then we created art. While we will never know exactly why our ancestors wandered into the deep bowels of Mother Earth and drew on cave walls, one theory connects their art with their spirituality.[15]

This possible expression of spirituality is found in the astonishing cave art in the Lascaux and Chauvet-Pont-d'Arc caves in France.

The walls of these caves teem with lions, bison, bulls, and mammoths. One animal, however, seems to have captivated the ancient artists more than others: the horse. Their likenesses populate Ice Age art. In the twenty-thousand-year span before humans began to settle into our modern concept of civilization, horses are the most frequently drawn animal by humans of the era.[16] Before humans captured images of God in mosaics, before we gathered our stories of our experience with God in scrolls that would eventually become the Holy Bible, before we laid the stones that would become great cathedrals, we communicated our awe through horses in art.

Lest I get too romantic about horses and humanity's relationship with them, I note that our ancestors who drew images of ancient horses also ate them. The fossil record indicates that for early humans, horses were useful in many ways, including art and lunch. Eventually, however, we saw horses for the complex creatures they are and allowed our relationship to grow and change. We domesticated them and rode them, two events that may or may not be interrelated. We allowed them to change our movement. Suddenly, we could ride a horse and move further over distances and see more of the world around us.

They also became our companions. The relationship between horse and human is unique. Maybe their complexities and endurance across the ages gives us some insight to our own souls and our relationship with God. Maybe a part of the human soul is inexplicably connected to horses and has been for ages.

My first moment on a horse is captured in a picture. I'm sitting on a mare at my grandparents' farm. Her name is Lady, and she has her young foal beside her. My father's hand, barely present, is holding me in place on her back, and I seem inquisitive about this creature I've been set upon— me in a mustard yellow shirt on a horse, a vast tree filling the background. The image is slightly out of focus; a moment two souls meet can't honestly be captured in all its sharpness. I'm holding my finger to my mouth, a three-year-old's wisdom that on the back of a horse words aren't the most important part of the relationship. My red Keds are rolled inward to Lady's body; and I'm turned away from the person holding me on her and toward her neck. I wonder if my toddler self is considering grabbing her mane, a skill my adult rider self uses on occasion to stay on a feisty horse. The image is on a shelf in my living room. All image. No words. None are needed.

People of faith, however, need words. We are, as we like to say, people of the Word. We read and study the Word of God in the books of the Bible. We pray with words of thanksgiving, intercession, and confession. We have centuries of writings, words offered by theologians explaining, as much as we can, God and a life of faith.

When used judiciously, our words are important. They explain concepts and ideas. They resonate and inspire and remind us. Words tell our stories. They provide familiarity in their rhythm and form. I think of what it is like to pray with a person in the latter stages of dementia, when the disease has stripped their ability to recognize close friends and family members, but the deep memories of prayers etched from decades of recitation allow them flawlessly to join in the words of long-familiar prayers: the Lord's Prayer, the Hail Mary, even the Jesus Prayer. The words have become infused with life and meaning. They are not simply filling space or allowing us to sound more intelligent than we are. They are part of our selves and souls, the bones of our faith to which eternity is attached.

Too often, however, our words of faith can devolve until we sound like the rambling uncle who comes to Thanksgiving dinner, ranting about the latest conspiracy theory he read on the Internet. They become the public headline for a private story that is the opposite. How many times have we heard, "I'm sorry for what I did," only to have the person's actions communicate how unrepentant they truly are.

Words can become the barbed wire we wrap around our deepest honesty, a barrier we use to separate our deep truth from what is acceptably edited to share with those who may or will judge us for our words of deep truth. Speaking our truth is an act of courage and defiance to the seductive ease of cheap grace and comfortable faith. Our culture of comfortable faith has phrases we love speckled with appropriate showing of tears, but it never delves into the holy messiness that rests deep within each of us and God.

Messy words, the words spoken with shaky timbre and often met with holy silence, are an entirely different matter. Maybe I am the only person with a tendency to distance myself from my emotions with words. When asked, "How do you feel?" about a tragic event, my initial impulse is to begin a dissertation on when bad things happen to good people and how God shines forth in the darkness. Answering with an essay question gives me a sense of control. It intellectualizes the beautiful mess of grief, sadness, and disappointment that feels too fearful to speak aloud.

"I'm scared" is a powerful, difficult statement to say to the universe. "I'm sad," "I'm grieving," "I'm hopeless," all announce our frailty to a world that seems far too powerful, too crushing for our human bones and tendons and spirits. If our words are honest and simple, the world will defeat us, we think. And sometimes the world does defeat us, push us into the ditch and leave us for dead. Many times, those sisters and brothers in the faith are the ones who kick the dirt on our battered bodies.

No wonder the essay-question responses filled with questionably honest words feel safe. No wonder we say, "I'm fine," when we often are anything but. No wonder we explain and edit the words Jesus spoke to prostitutes and other nasty women and men to make them G-rated when they are anything but. Our words often belie our feelings as an act of self-preservation. These words and the marginal truth they contain float in the air, not grounded in our true feelings and emotions, because wounded souls are too often prey in a predatory culture.

I'd experienced this predatory culture firsthand and still had a few wounds healing when I arrived in Lexington. My first years of ministry and, quite honestly, most of my life had been dedicated to polishing my good-girl persona to a stellar shine. Nod and smile, even when your dignity is bludgeoned. Strive to match people's expectations, even at the expense of my own truth. Say, "I'm fine," and keep saying it until it feels true.

I discovered the words never did ring true to my deepest soul. My constant refrains of "I'm fine" drowned out the part of my self and soul that needed desperately to speak the truth. So I did, and I was almost eaten alive by those who cared more about my silence in the church than words of honesty.

I had a decision. I could stay where words alone mattered, or I could move and shift to a deeper place. I could move away from the place I'd stood in for too long and rediscover God and, in that same place, my own truthful messy words.

Imagine my surprise when, in this place where I found this messy God, I also rediscovered horses.

My eternal but inconsistent relationship with God and horses changed significantly when I moved to Kentucky. My relationship with God was finding a new expression—one that did not find words as helpful as they once had been.

It was then that I learned how the prose of faith is not the only way to experience of God. The narratives, treatises, sermons, and tracts express ideas, and yet they also may constrain the expansiveness of God in paragraphs and punctuation.

Did you know that the original texts of the Bible lacked capitalization and punctuation and, to some extent, structure as we know it in our English translations? Biblical Hebrew, Aramaic, and Greek looked like an e.e. cummings poem gone amuck on the page. Our original words of faith were a miasma of narrative, image, mystery, and poetry. They expressed glorious refrains and gut-wrenching agony. They were raw and full of feeling that could hardly be contained.

Yet, through the centuries, we've all but smothered these poetic, emotion-filled words with expressions of constancy. The stiff upper lips of our souls read aloud the agony of the Cross and the alleluia of the Resurrection with the same tone and tenor.

Give God enough time, I've discovered in a comfortable and steady life, and God will lead you into the desert where you're quite sure you've been abandoned. In that place of barrenness, we rediscover the poetry of our faith. The words of the agony of the Cross are the blood crying from the soil of our ancient soul. The alleluia of the Resurrection is a sharp intake of breath, followed by tears of joy and release.

Give God enough time, and God will lead you, as God led me back to horses, back to the three-year-old who wore red shoes and held her finger over her mouth to stop using so many words, to stop intellectually explaining so much. Who instead listened to feelings and expressed herself with crayons, maybe a horse drawn on the wall of my home. Back to the part of my tiny, ancient soul, who finally got to do what eons of humans have done—have a relationship with a horse. God led me back to God's magnificent creatures who speak in poetry, not prose, and who respond, not to diatribes, but to simple shifts in the physical body and in clicks and kisses, where "Because I ride Izzy" has all the words I need to say.

Give God enough time, and God will entice us to listen to the wisdom of shifts and silence, of movement and stillness, of the poetry of horses.

ACKNOWLEDGMENTS

I have eternal gratitude to the faithful community of writers who help and affirm via social media and email; and to the many friends who read drafts, listen to me whine about my own self-doubt as a writer, and drag me away from the writing process when needed to discuss matters of true import like the latest BBC costume drama (Brad); shoes and puppies (Mary); or all things frozen yogurt, cowgirls, and faith in God's love (Karen, Anita, and Michele respectively).

A special acknowledgment to Meredith Gould, who believed in this book before I did and gave me the courage and guidance to write it.

Writing also comes from a nourished soul, and I cannot give thanks enough to the Church of St. Michael the Archangel and the faithful, courageous, and loving members who gather week after week to celebrate Christ's love and who work to share that love in the world. Thank you for realizing that riding helps me be a better priest and affirming the value of self-care. Thank you for being the community of faith where I serve as your priest. Thank you for listening to many sermons about horses and God.

For all the ways horses draw me back to myself, they are not the only way I remember who I am. Thanks to the wonderful friends of Chelsea Pines Country Club and Doggie Day Spa (as we've named our friends' home) for pool time, puppy time, and friends time. My dog Evie especially appreciates playtime when I'm trying to write.

This book would not be possible without the many people and horses who help me ride. My appreciation and love for Wingswept Farm in Nicholasville, Kentucky, is endless. It is where I ride and learn about horses. It is where I have a wonderful barn family. It is where I come home to myself. I count myself blessed to have Stephanie and Chris Brannan, the owners and trainers of Wingswept Farm, in my life as a rider and as a person. Any errors or incorrect statements about riding technique or horses are mine alone and are not a reflection of their vast knowledge of horses—training, riding, and showing them. Thank you, also, to all the people and groups who share the story of the American Saddlebred. They are truly magnificent horses; when we ride them, we soar.

I have deep gratitude for all the wonderful riders at Wingswept, also known as the Barn Family. I know no other group of people with whom I'd rather shovel horse poop or live this amazing, slightly crazy horse lifestyle. Not a week goes by that my barn family doesn't remind me of the deep value of having people who love you just as you are, especially when you're covered in horse hair.

The horses at Wingswept also get a big thank-you for all the wisdom you share with me. The horses I mention are all very real, although I have changed some names. I couldn't include every reflection and every moment I've learned something about God or myself from you horses at the barn, but believe me, I hear how you speak of God, too. The carrots and apples will be in your feed buckets soon.

And of course, thanks to Nina. Lucky girls get their own pony, and luckier women get their own horse. To love and be loved by a horse . . . it is a feeling not to be captured by words.

NOTES

1   Smith Lilly, *Saddle Seat Horsemanship: A Complete Guide to Riding, Training and Showing* (n.p., 2012), 59.

2   Yvette Grant, ed., *The Little Red Book of Horse Wisdom* (New York: Skyhorse Publishing 2012), 152.

3   Saddlebred Horse Division, 2013 United States Equestrian Federation Rule Book (PDF). United States Equestrian Federation, Rule SB102, retrieved January 30, 2013.

4   "Gospel of Thomas saying 70," http://gnosis.org/naghamm/ gosthom.html, accessed January 31, 2017.

5   Parker Palmer, *Let Your Life Speak: Listening for the Voice of Vocation* (San Francisco: Jossey-Bass, 2000), 10.

6   Derek Olsen, *Inwardly Digest: The Prayer Book as Guide to a Spiritual Life* (Cincinnati: Forward Movement, 2016), 143.

7   Lilly, *Saddle Seat Horsemanship*, 41.

8   Hal M. Helms, e.d., *The Practice of the Presence of God by Brother Lawrence: A New Translation by Robert J. Edmonson* (Brewster, MA: Paraclete Press, 1985), 100.

9   Janet Jones, "Visual Discrepancies," *Equus*, 462 (March 2016): 50.

10 Grant, *Little Red Book*, 86.

11 Rainer Maria Rilke, *Letters to a Young Poet* (Mineola, NY: Dover, 2002), 39.

12 Richard Rohr, https://cac.org/in-need-of-healing-2016-05-29/, accessed December 10, 2017.

13 Mother Columba Hart, OSB, *Hadewich: The Complete Works* (Mahwah, NJ: Paulist Press, 1980), 213.

14 Thomas P. McDonnell, ed., *A Thomas Merton Reader* (New York: Image Books, 1989), 386.

15 "Meanings of the Paleolithic Cave Art of France," http://www.bradshawfoundation.com/clottes/meanings.php, accessed January 31, 2017.

16 Wendy Williams, *The Horse: The Epic History of our Noble Companions* (New York: Scientific American, 2015), 14.

ABOUT PARACLETE PRESS

WHO WE ARE

As the publishing arm of the Community of Jesus, Paraclete Press presents a full expression of Christian belief and practice—from Catholic to Evangelical, from Protestant to Orthodox, reflecting the ecumenical charism of the Community and its dedication to sacred music, the fine arts, and the written word. We publish books, recordings, sheet music, and DVDs that nourish the vibrant life of the church and its people.

WHAT WE ARE DOING

Books

PARACLETE PRESS BOOKS show the richness and depth of what it means to be Christian. While Benedictine spirituality is at the heart of who we are and all that we do, our books reflect the Christian experience across many cultures, time periods, and houses of worship.

We have many series, including *Paraclete Essentials; Paraclete Fiction; Paraclete Giants*; and the new *The Essentials of...*, devoted to Christian classics. Others include *Voices from the Monastery* (men and women monastics writing about living a spiritual life today), *Active Prayer*, the award-winning *Paraclete Poetry*, and new for young readers: *The Pope's Cat*. We also specialize in gift books for children on the occasions of Baptism and First Communion, as well as other important times in a child's life, and books that bring creativity and liveliness to any adult spiritual life.

The MOUNT TABOR BOOKS series focuses on the arts and literature as well as liturgical worship and spirituality; it was created in conjunction with the Mount Tabor Ecumenical Centre for Art and Spirituality in Barga, Italy.

Music

The PARACLETE RECORDINGS label represents the internationally acclaimed choir *Gloriæ Dei Cantores*, the *Gloriæ Dei Cantores Schola*, and the other instrumental artists of the *Arts Empowering Life Foundation*.

Paraclete Press is the exclusive North American distributor for the Gregorian chant recordings from St. Peter's Abbey in Solesmes, France. Paraclete also carries all of the Solesmes chant publications for Mass and the Divine Office, as well as their academic research publications.

In addition, PARACLETE PRESS SHEET MUSIC publishes the work of today's finest composers of sacred choral music, annually reviewing over 1,000 works and releasing between 40 and 60 works for both choir and organ.

Video

Our DVDs offer spiritual help, healing, and biblical guidance for a broad range of life issues including grief and loss, marriage, forgiveness, facing death, understanding suicide, bullying, addictions, Alzheimer's, and Christian formation.

Learn more about us at our website:
www.paracletepress.com or phone us toll-free at 1.800.451.5006

SCAN
TO
READ
MORE

Glory Happening:
Finding the Divine in Everyday Places
Kaitlin Curtice
$15.99 Trade paper | ISBN 978-1-61261-896-8
"With the insights of a prophet and the attention of
a poet, Kaitlin Curtice invites the reader to see the
world fresh, in all its everyday glory. You will never
look at a sink of dishes, a mound of dough, a game
of Rummy, or the family dog the same way again.
A stunner of a debut, every sentence a feast for the
senses." —Rachel Held Evans, author of *Searching for
Sunday*

Everbloom:
Stories of Deeply Rooted and Transformed Lives
Women of Redbud Writers Guild
$17.00 Trade paper | ISBN 978-1-61261-933-0
"We read to see elements of our own hearts,
experiences and stories reflected back to us in the
words of others. This collection is just that: stories that
help us feel seen, known, and understood. Honestly
and beautifully told, this book will keep you in good
company along your own journey." —Shauna Niequist,
author of *Present Over Perfect*

At Home in This Life:
*Finding Peace at the Crossroads of Unraveled Dreams
and Beautiful Surprises*
Jerusalem Jackson Greer
$18.99 Trade paper | ISBN 978-1-61261-632-2
"I love Jerusalem's realness, her willingness to walk
us through her own story and show us how it mimics
a universal story we all know in our bones: God is
good, even when things end up differently than how
we thought they would. Her wit, candor, and love of
ancient practices woke up my bones to a renewed
sense of wonder at how God is at work around us all
the time, in ways big and small. Her ordinary life is a
gift, because it's full of the magic of God—just like all
our lives." —Tsh Oxenreider, author of *At Home in the
World* and *Notes from a Blue Bike*

Available through most booksellers or through Paraclete Press:
www.paracletepress.com | 1-800-451-5006
Try your local bookstore first.